COACHING
WINNING
BASEBALL

COACHING WINNING BASEBALL

DELL
BETHEL

Photos By
Marvin L. Axelrod

Contemporary Books, Inc.
Chicago

Library of Congress Cataloging in Publication Data

Bethel, Dell.
    Coaching winning baseball.

    Includes index.
    1. Baseball coaching.   2. Baseball—Defense.
3. Baseball—Offense.   I. Title.
GV875.5.B47 1979   796.357′077   78-73659
ISBN 0-8092-7460-4
ISBN 0-8092-7459-0 pbk.

Copyright © 1979 by Dell Bethel
All rights reserved
Published by Contemporary Books, Inc.
180 North Michigan Avenue, Chicago, Illinois 60601
Manufactured in the United States of America
Library of Congress Catalog Card Number: 78-73659
International Standard Book Number: 0-8092-7460-4 (cloth)
                       0-8092-7459-0 (paper)
Published simultaneously in Canada
Beaverbooks
953 Dillingham Road
Pickering, Ontario L1W 1Z7
Canada

This book is dedicated to my loyal wife Polly who through the years has been a splendid third base coach, and to our son, Bill, the enthusiastic first base coach, who has always given me the hit away sign for being in the profession of coaching. Also to all the young people it has been my joy and privilege to coach for the past twenty-five years.

Contents

Acknowledgments

I wish to acknowledge the great baseball players, coaches, and managers I have had the pleasure to play under or work with side by side. I have learned much of what I have written in the pages to follow from these men, who through their love and dedication have made baseball the great game it is today.

These men are William Leslie Bethel, Fred Warburton, Ray Ross, Ed Burke, Dick Siebert, Ray Gestaut, Angelo Giuliani, Andy Gilbert, Carl Hubbell, Bubber Jonnard, Paul Deese, Ron Oestrike, George Medich, Chick Genovese, Tom Heath, Jack Fisher, Leo Durocher, Don Kirsch, Cliff Dorow, John Kasper, Dave Kosher, Larry Starr, Al Campanis, Grady Hatton, Jim Fitzharris, Rosy Ryan, Don Pries, Charlie Fox, Chuck Tanner, Rollie Hemond, Bill Veeck, Hal Middlesworth, Ed Katalinas, Rich Rollins, Ralph Kiner, Charlie Lau, John Sain, Wally Moses, Whitey Herzog, Dick Howser, George Brophy, Eddie Yost, Ray Berres, Brooks Robinson, Clete Boyer, Bud Harrelson, Mickey McConnell, Cliff Kachline, Harry Walker, Ted Williams, and Andy Cohen.

I also wish to express my sincere appreciation to Herman Masin, editor of *Scholastic Coach,* for his encouragement and assistance in my writing endeavors from the beginning.

Introduction

Dell Bethel and Vern Ruhle

Coach Bethel made me feel I could make it in the major leagues. His teaching approach to the mental aspects of this game helped me become a winning pitcher.

Dell knows the mechanics of pitching and is a real student of the game. He helped change my grip and style of pitching, so all my pitches now have movement. He is one of the best pitching coaches in the country.

Nothing can replace the desire to play the game. Desire is the key to discipline. Dell instilled the desire and discipline I needed to make the major leagues. With his enthusiasm and love for the game, he taught me the value of *fun* in baseball.

Vern Ruhle, Pitcher
Houston Astros

1

What Makes a Great Coach?

What makes a great coach? Many years ago as a young coach I posed this question to an outstanding coach I worked for. He had spent all his life working with young people and was not only an outstanding coach but had a tremendous influence on the people he worked with. His answer is a universal truth which still applies today.

"*The most important ingredient in winning coaching is good material.* With it you can have an outstanding team; without it your team can only reach a certain level of development."

You can become the best coach possible if you follow certain principles that will bring the best out of your team and you.

First you must coach and teach according to your personality. Some coaches are quiet by nature, some are in between, and others are holler guys. If you coach the way your personality is, you will be much more effective. Your players will know you are honest with them, and that feeling will be transmitted to them. A team becomes a reflection of you. One of the great satisfactions in coaching is that you can teach and see a player develop again and again. A playing career may be short in years, but you can coach as long as the desire is there to do it. You can repeat it year after year with new young men.

What makes an outstanding coach? Basically, judgment of a coach's performance must include his ability, conditions and relative resources, and the use he makes of the means at his disposal.

Let's examine each of these factors a little closer. Ability is almost undefinable, as each person's ability is as individual as his personality. Certain characteristics should be present, however. A coach should be a strong figure who has gained the respect of his players. How does

Rocco Scotti sings the national anthem with his whole heart before a game in Cleveland.

Everyone is important in this game. Making them feel that way is an important part of your job. This grounds keeper gets a standing ovation in Detroit. The people love him there.

he do this? With confidence in himself and complete knowledge of his sport, the coach is the leader with the courage of his own convictions. He is able to make quick decisions and act upon them *without fearing the consequences.* Making the crucial decision at the crucial time wins. It is the ability to put into motion the unexpected move that upsets the opponent's balance without upsetting your own team.

As a leader, the coach builds strength of character as well as mental attitude in his players. Flexibility in decision-making, ready acceptance of responsibility, and independence of thought are good building blocks. When provided with this as a strong foundation, players will be able to make solid decisions without being pushed to the wall by fear.

The coach must establish personal contact with his players without losing the least measure of authority. Establishment of idealism raises the performance of each player to a superior level, with fear and anxiety kept to a minimum. The coach develops a spirit of camaraderie; the team works together in spirit and body, with each member doing his part in the joint effort. Motivation, preparation through practice and hard work, and good decision-making along with ability, respect for the human spirit, and confidence in a good coach give each player the tools necessary to win.

Conditions and raw material are usually uncontrollable factors for the coach. Yet, these given factors are his greatest limitations. Casey Stengel worked for years with many teams and players, but never got out of the cellar. Given the right conditions and players, he revolutionized the game of baseball with his platooning, and became one of the greatest managers in the world. He never changed a thing he did; only the uncontrollable factors changed. He had the material to build. These success factors can be present anywhere: from small towns like Bad Axe, where one call brings a player to the only phone in town, to Stengel's New York City.

Recognize the conditions you're dealing with; don't ask a team to do more than it is capable of doing. You don't set impossible goals; you must work within the framework of the given players' abilities. The coach sticks with his players regardless of the results and is proud of his team when each member has truly put forth his best effort. Furthermore, he tells them so, regardless of the score. *It is better to build boys than to mend men.* Making the most of the resources you have is probably the greatest challenge for a coach and also the most rewarding. Seeing one of his players make the majors is the ultimate reward for a coach, but this is for but a few. *A coach must be satisfied with getting the best from each player and with recognizing it as the best. Helping a boy reach his own goals can be an immediate reward, but often the finale comes in five, ten, or fifteen years, when the coach sees his player in the role chosen for life.* One way of measuring the leadership of a coach is the extent to which his team impresses the opposition. Not always have the winners been remembered: Napoleon, Lee, Hannibal, and Rommel were downed by defeat, yet in history rise above their conquerors.

I firmly believe that *leadership* is the key to becoming a great coach. The people who study human behavior tell us that only *five percent* of the people in the world are *leaders.* In studying managers, coaches, and great people in all walks of life I find that the real leaders seldom talk about why they are leaders. They have the talent of leadership. Some of the great hitters can wear the ball out but can't tell you how they do it. They just hit.

Over the years I've observed and studied people who are real leaders and have come up with principles that, if you incorporate them in your teaching and coaching, will make you a real leader, outstanding coach, image of a real man to your players, and developer of young people.

1. Develop a complete knowledge of the technical side of baseball—how to teach the game—and understand the importance of having organizational expertise.
   a.) Once you've accomplished this you will have confidence in your own knowledge.
   b.) Organizational expertise will help you get the most out of your teams' time and efforts.

2. Create an independence of mind, so that you don't have to imitate or follow blindly another great coach, never questioning the principles he operates under. If you have a solid foundation in what you know about the game and you are not inhibited in your thinking, you then are free to question basic principles and come up with some innovative and creative ideas of your own. *Think for yourself.*

3. Mental conception must be followed by execution. This is where we run into people who are dreamers but not leaders. They conceive ideas but don't follow through on what needs to be done. What can be conceived in your mind can be achieved. Young coaches must learn that just as much energy and hard work is required of them as mental ability. The sensational victory or upset is more often than not largely a victory for the energy and hard work of the coaches and the team.

National anthem, Cleveland.

4. Players have a fine spirit of idealism. Coaches should never forget this and must try to do all they can to maintain and preserve this idealism in their players.

   a.) Make each and every member of your team feel important. This is a crucial part of your job.

   b.) Strive for excellence; today average performance is everywhere accepted as satisfactory. You can challenge the young people to shoot for the stars.

   c.) You have a real opportunity to influence some of these young people for the rest of their lives. Some do not have fathers or come from broken homes and are looking for a male image. You can make your impression, a real positive one, and turn out winning human beings as well as winning teams.

5. The coach by personal example plays the principal role in increasing the performance his players will give. They watch your every move, how you conduct yourself in relation to your umpires, for example. If you treat them respectfully, your players will. Are you fair with everyone? Do you require everyone to do the same conditioning? Do you work hard and not cry about bad breaks or bad weather? If so, your players will develop mental toughness and a real fighting spirit. Do you try to come up with new ideas which will upset the other team? (seven-man infield on bunt situations, four-man outfield for a power hitter?) This type of thinking will develop in your players confidence in you as a coach. Confidence increases in direct proportion to the amount of time and hard work put into an endeavor. By doing these things, you as a coach can increase the performance of your players enormously. This gives you a superior instrument with which you can accomplish far more tactically than your opponent. Your players then want to do their best for you because they regard you as a real *leader*.

6. Know your opponent, especially the rival coach. When the game starts, each coach has his own plan on how he would like to play the game. Your team, unless you have overwhelmingly better material, will have to

The Yankee coaching staff talks over its plans before the big game. (Bob Lemon, Dick Howser, and Yogi Berra)

be flexible. (Does your opponent like to squeeze, play for one run early in the game, hit and run, steal whenever possible? What defenses do they employ?)

7. Great leaders all seem to have photographic minds in relation to their fields of endeavor. Rommel, Napoleon, Casey Stengel all had this, as did Leo Durocher. It is a trait you can develop and it pays real dividends. You can make great strides in this with intense concentration and interest. You will be surprised how fast a coach can pick up this talent.

8. Great coaches develop great physical conditioning programs.

   a.) Often you will beat a team simply because you are in better condition.

   b.) An individual player will never reach his full potential until he is in his best possible physical condition.

   c.) By being in top condition you will cut down on injuries.

   d.) Condition your players mentally to be as tough as possible by practicing in rain and in cold on occasion. You will play games under these conditions, and often you can defeat a far superior opponent who simply does not want to play under these game conditions.

Dell Bethel and Dick Howser talk baseball on the field.

9. Think for yourself so that you can see all the possibilities in a situation, be it in practice or a game.
    a.) Don't become bound by tradition or play by the book all the time. Be inventive.
10. The real leader and coach must have mental gifts of a high order as well as great strength of character to fulfill his job.
    a.) There are so many possibilities in a baseball game today that it is tough to make more than a rough forecast of how the game will unfold.
    b.) The game will be decided by your flexibility of mind.
    c.) Be willing to accept responsibility.
        1.) You will make the change of pitchers.
        2.) Don't put a boy in the third base coaching box when you can be there.
        3.) Make the decision when to walk the man intentionally.
11. Everyone, coaches and players, must be pulling together. Your team must have unity of purpose—the spirit and will to pull together. Anything or anyone which may detract from this must be utterly eradicated.
12. Finally, try to take your team and make the members feel like a family. If you develop this feeling, you will have high morale and *esprit de corps* on your team.
13. It is my belief that any man who sets himself up as a coach should accept without reservation every pupil who comes to him for instruction. The coach is a teacher. This is a policy with which many of my colleagues do not agree, since the man who subscribes to it lays himself open to the acceptance of much unpromising material. So what? I once asked a painter, who today is one of the world's foremost artists. "How do you know which paintings in your work will become masterpieces or your best pieces of work?" He turned the question around a la Socrates and said, "How do you know which one of these boys you are working with will become another Stottlemyre?"

You do your best, and sometimes everything falls in place—and you have something better than you ever dreamed of. The coach's job is to help the athlete to improve, and he should be prepared to accept any challenge to his professional prestige. No athlete is so good or so bad that sound coaching will not make him better, and in the circles that matter, a coach's reputation rests more on his success with the undistinguished many than with the illustrious few. Though the majority of athletes never become professionals or national champions or even local champions, your interest in each should be no less than in the major leaguer. Every one of them is capable of improvement, often to a far greater extent than you or they may realize. It is the coach's privilege to bring this about and to share the deep satisfaction it brings, however insignificant it may be by higher standards.

If you put these specific principles to work in your coaching, you should be a real leader, a winning coach who helps develop winning human beings. In closing this chapter, I would like to share a quote from a major league player's handbook which to me expresses the whole philosophy of the profession of coaching:

> You may not know the kids in this area, but they know you. . . . Don't disappoint them by smoking in front of them or by acting like anything but a gentleman. You are their Hero, and they worship you and your abilities.

Lou Gehrig had this poem on his dresser and tried to live by it. A great philosophy of coaching:

That Little Chap

A careful man I want to be.
A little fellow follows me.
I do not dare to go astray
For fear he'll go the self-same way.

I cannot once escape his eye
Whate'er he sees me do, he tries,
Like me, he says he's going to be,
That little chap who follows me.

He thinks that I am big and fine,
Believes in every word of mine.
The base in me he must not see,
That little chap who follows me.

I must remember as I go.
Through summer suns and winter snows,
I'm building for the years to be
That little chap who follows me.

Billy Martin. One of the attributes of a great coach or manager is that he coaches and doesn't worry about the consequences.

2

Picking and Building Your Team

In picking your team, there are certain things you should look for in your players. First are the physical qualifications; second, the mental qualifications; third, morale and hustle; and fourth, desire to play.

Let's look at these individually. One physical qualification that will help a player both offensively and defensively is speed. This becomes a crucial factor, especially if you like to play a running style of game. What kind of arm does the player have? Have your outfielders throw to home plate. If the throw picks up speed after the hop to the plate, the outfielder has a good arm. If it slows up like a dying quail, his arm needs development.

Have all your infielders throw from the hole at shortstop, and you can quickly evaluate their arms. A side note here: many times a young player will have a quick release; even though his arm isn't as strong as another candidate's, the

ball will get to first base quicker. It is easy for a coach to make this mistake (likewise on the double play). When in doubt, put a stop watch on each player to see how long it takes for the ball to reach first on the same play.

The size of hands is a positive factor, especially if the player has very large ones. Sandy Koufax and Johnny Bench can hold six baseballs in one hand with the palm facing up. In a pitcher, size of hands is one of the first things I look at, along with the length of the arms.

If the player's arms hanging straight down are long enough to scratch his knees without bending over, then he has real leverage. Don't become locked into one of these attributes, though, as there have been many successful pitchers and baseball players with short arms and fingers.

Physical size is important and can help in the power department, but it is not a must. Baseball is a game where a small man can really excel. Freddie Patek is living proof of this. Sometimes you as a coach have to sell a young man who thinks that he is too small that he can really be a top-notch player.

Mental ability: look for boys who use their heads for something besides a cap rack, boys who want to pick your brains to improve themselves and learn everything they can about this game.

Hustle: does the player hustle as hard as he can, and does he play aggressively? Is he a Pete Rose type of player? When a player has the real desire to play, it will cover a multitude of sins. This will carry him far beyond some fellows who have superior ability.

Let's go to the field for your team try-outs. Ask each player what position he likes to play and put him in that position. Let him show what he can do in that position. Bear in mind you may later shift him to another position. Connie Mack said many years ago that "A real baseball player can just about play any position on the diamond," and I think there is a lot of truth in it. If you ask a player to try another position, suggest that you would like to see him work at the position. Make the player feel that he may become even greater at the other position. This confidence and rapport is important with young men and boys; they are sensitive. A kind word and a pat on the back when it is sincere will go far in getting the most out of your players.

Remember, animal trainers are probably the greatest teachers in the world, and often even their lives depend on their teaching methods. When working with the big cats and bears the *key to their success is that they always regard their charges with a kind word or a treat when they perform well.*

How do you build your team after watching the players?

First, you must be "strong up the middle." I firmly believe that if you have strong pitching and catching, your team can challenge a top level team on any given day no matter how small your school or little league team. Learn as much as you can about the art of pitching and catching so you can give your players the fine points of this aspect of the game.

Your catcher should be fairly well built with a lot of bulldog in him. A key play I use to evaluate my catchers is the play at the plate with a runner coming in full barrel. If your catcher stays in there, comes up with the throw, and hangs onto it, he has the makings of a good one. I have found over the years that the catcher who lets the throw get by him or muffs it doesn't like the contact, and you will end up losing close ball games because of it. Your catcher has to be a hard worker with real hustle. It is a tough position, but if the catcher is outstanding, he can advance quickly in baseball.

Pitchers come in all shapes and sizes, but they must be real competitors who love battling and facing challenges. Someone who is a real flame thrower and can bring heat is a natural pitcher. You may have to develop his control, a key in pitching. Another important aspect of pitching is the ability of your pitchers to make their pitches move.

Spend a great deal of time with your pitchers. They can keep you in any ball game. Strive to develop a smooth working double play combination. It is one of the most beautiful plays in baseball, and executing crucial double plays will make poor pitching look better—and fair pitching look excellent.

Your shortstop should be the best fielder on your team. He should have a great arm and tremendous ability to go to his right or left, field the ball, and make the throw, if need be from almost any position. The real test for any shortstop is the hard hit ball to his right, just out of reach of the third baseman. If he can consistently get the ball and throw the runner out at first base, you have a great one. Your second baseman should be a good pivot man on the double play, but his arm need not be as strong as your shortstop's. In baseball, there is a saying that the double play is made with your stomach. Your second baseman must have the guts to stay in there when he is going to get hit by the base runner. A few years ago there was an outstanding Major League prospect who simply didn't have the stomach for the double play and consequently couldn't make it, even though he had all the tools.

In your center fielder, look for a boy who has a strong throwing arm and excellent running

Pete Rose from the left side. You can build your team around players with this type of hustle and ability. Where would you bat him in your lineup, coach?

speed. He must also be a sure catcher of fly balls, not one with cement hands. Running speed will help him cover the large territory at center, and the great hose for an arm will keep the baserunners honest. Most young players can be taught to become good flyhawks.

This completes your strength up the middle. Catcher, pitcher, shortstop, second baseman, center fielder—the core of great defense.

On the flanks you have two outfield positions, first base and third base to fill. In some of these positions you will place your better hitters, if everything else is equal.

If possible, put right-handed throwers in left and center field and your left-handed thrower in right field. The reason is that a lot of their throws will come on plays to the foul lines, and they won't have to make that big turn before throwing.

You like your first baseman to have height, reach, and agility along with good hands. Preferably, he should be a left-handed thrower.

Your third baseman should have a good arm, catlike quickness in handling hard hit balls, and a howitzer for an arm if possible.

Overall for your team, look for a nice balance offensively and defensively. Offensively you will want to be able to have a balanced number of right- and left-handed hitters.

You sacrifice hitting at shortstop, if need be, to give you a great defensive player. If players are equal, you go with the player who is a better hitter. We like to give a very high priority on our teams to running speed. We like to put pressure on the defense by knowing that we will run, take the extra base, steal, and try to make things happen.

It is now time to hand the line-up card to the umpire. Give your batting order some careful thought.

Your Batting Order:

No. 1: Speed, great judge of strike zone, a hitter with real talent for getting on base to get something started.

No. 2: Should be able to bunt and hit to the opposite field on the hit and run. Good speed and can consistently make contact with the ball.

No. 3: Best hitter for average who can run.

No. 4: Clean-up hitter, power man.

No. 5: Another power hitter if you are fortunate enough to have two.

No. 6: Consistent hitter.

Nos. 7 and 8: Your weakest hitters.

No. 9: Your weakest link; he must learn how to bunt for base hits.

TIPS FOR YOU, THE COACH

1. Try to get one solid unit. Let team members play together as much as possible.
2. Try experimenting with the depth at which your infield plays. Many young teams play their infields way too deep, and even if a player comes up with the ball and makes a perfect throw, the runner beats it out.
   a.) In a high school game you might count the number of topped or slow hit ground balls that are hit in the infield and how tough it is for the infielder who is playing too deep to make the play.
3. Young boys' games are often seven, six, or five innings in length. Remember, you are actually starting in the third, fourth, or fifth inning of a nine-inning game; adjust your thinking accordingly.
4. If you score one run, it takes two to beat you; if you get two, it takes three to beat you. In short games, this becomes a real factor.
5. The lower the classification of baseball, the more you should run. The great coach prepares not only his players for the game of baseball, but also for the game of life.

part 1
The Defense in Baseball

3

Mastering Control: The Key to Pitching

What is the key to pitching? *Control.* How do you teach control? How can a pitcher be improved in this area? What is real control in pitching?

In recent years I have come to believe that the mental aspect of pitching has a great deal to do with control. Even on the major league level, you may have noticed that a pitcher may be struggling along and be wild and perhaps walk one or two hitters, but as soon as there are some base runners his control becomes much sharper and he doesn't have any trouble finding the strike zone. I believe the big reason for this change is the pitcher's mental attitude. Now, instead of trying to overpower the hitter and blow it by him, he wants to fool the hitter, getting him off-balance so he will hit out in front of the pitch or behind it. The result is often a ground ball for a double play or a pop

up. His main idea now is to fool the man with the lumber at the plate, either by taking a little off the pitch or putting a little more on it.

There are several ways of improving a pitcher's control. I like to use the examples of the golfer and bird hunter. A golfer who aims right at the pin on a green has a much better chance of hitting the larger green area, even if he misses the very small actual target, the pin. The same concept applies to pitching—by aiming at a small target you may miss the actual target but still get a strike. I use the bird hunter analogy to point out that a hunter reacts instinctively in aiming his rifle and firing as the birds are flushed. Many pitchers do develop this pattern of trying to carefully aim the ball over the plate.

Control is more than the ability to throw in the strike zone; it also entails mastery of the

13

1

2

3

6

7

11

12

4

5

9

10

13

Sparky Lyle, one of the really great pitchers of our time. A real power pitcher with a master's control of his fast ball and hard slider, his bread and butter pitches. Notice in photos 1–7 Lyle's powerful thrust and push-off from the rubber. Photo 8 shows the perfect arm position as his front foot is planted. This is the key position in control and pitching. If the pitcher is in this position at this point in his delivery, his pitching mechanics are right. Note in photos 9 and 10 how Sparky has buried his throwing shoulder toward the ground. This allows for maximum power in a pitcher's fast ball. In photo 13, he is ready to field anything hit his direction.

corners and the low strike. The strike low and away comes closest to being the unhittable pitch.

Relaxation at all times is a must. For example, most young pitchers grip the baseball much too tightly, especially with the thumb, which destroys good wrist action and creates arm tension. Try this yourself by gripping a ball hard with the thumb—notice the difference in the range of movement of your wrist and hand. We like to tell our pitchers to think of a ball as an egg while gripping it. To assist in relaxation, take a deep breath before pitching. A pitcher should know what pitch has been signaled for and where it should be delivered. Concentration toward delivery of the pitch should be keen. If a pitcher can do this about one hundred times a game, he should be a consistent winner.

SOME OTHER AIDS IN GAINING CONTROL

Try to split the heart of the plate with a low first pitch (possibly aiming at your catcher's crotch). If you have your good stuff that day, the ball should take off and catch one of the corners. Many professional pitchers try to be too fine in aiming the ball for a corner of the plate. If they just miss, they are in the hole. Falling behind in the count leads to real control problems; then you have to either come in with a real fat pitch or walk the hitter.

Always throw at a target. This requires concentrated effort. Satchel Paige developed control by practicing with a matchbox for a plate. If he could cut the corners of the small matchbox, home plate would appear to be a very large and easy target to hit after pitching at one so small.

Try to visualize the anticipated path or groove of the pitch before delivering.

Start with the pivot foot on the middle of the rubber. If your pitch is wild inside or outside, simply move over on the rubber and keep using the same motion.

When you are wild high, you are releasing the

Ron Guidry, the classic lefthander who was the best pitcher in baseball for 1978, won 27 games, lost only 3. Ron has fantastic arm speed, somewhere between 600 to 700 miles per hour just before reaching his release point (notice the blur caused by his arm speed in photo 12 from the stretch). His arm speed, coupled with his ability to get his body totally behind the pitch in a very smooth, fluid, and powerful motion, is why he is able to throw his fast ball up to speeds of 100 miles per hour even though he only weighs 155 pounds.

4

 1

 2

 3

 5

 6

 7

 9

 10

 1

Notice how he really buries his pitching shoulder into the ground in photos 16, 17, and 18 from the wind-up and photo 13 from the stretch.

Also note how he literally explodes and jumps at the hitter, letting his whole body go into the pitch to get that little extra on each delivery. It is very apparent in photo 19 from the wind-up and photo 16 from the stretch.

Being an all-around athlete (Ron has run the 100-yard dash in 9.7 seconds) and having great spring in his legs help him to do a splendid job of fielding his position. Note in the last photo from the wind-up and from the stretch his perfect fielding position. He is ready to spring like a cat in any direction, including straight up for a high hopper.

Both photo sequences truly show poetry in motion. Especially note in photos 16–19 from the wind-up how freely the back leg is allowed to follow through with no strain on the body.

12

16

17

ball too soon. When you are wild low, you are holding the ball too long.

Develop a groove so that your lead foot lands in the same spot every time—don't become a scatter foot. Sandy Koufax could warm up twenty minutes and yet only leave one mark with his striding foot.

Throw each pitch from the same angle. Use your natural throwing motion on all pitches.

Work with one pitch at a time (first the fast ball, then the curve, etc.) until you can place it anywhere in the strike zone.

Learn first to throw at the catcher's mitt, then his shoulders, knees, and finally the lettering on his uniform.

Use the plate in practice, throwing at the corners.

Know where every pitch is going and why it is going there.

Keep your head up and still.

When pitching with men on base, be certain you have picked your target before starting your motion to the plate.

Spend half of your time in practice throwing from the stretch.

Draw a seven-foot line from your pivot foot

13 14 15

18 19

toward home plate. On the delivery (if you are a right-handed pitcher), your left leg should always end up on the left of this line. This will prevent you from throwing across your body.

Discipline yourself mentally. Anger destroys your concentration.

Throw the ball hard, don't aim it.

Run, run, and run some more. Lack of control late in the game is usually attributable to poor physical condition.

Chart every pitch you throw in practice and games (after you are warmed up). This will give you the facts in regard to your control.

20

1

2

Ron Guidry from the stretch.

6

7

8

12

13

14

3

4

5

9

10

11

15

16

1

John Hiller, premier Detroit relief pitcher. In pictures 12, 13, and 14, John is really burying that shoulder. In the last picture he has really let his body go to get that little extra on the pitch.

1

5

6

7

11

12

13

2

3

4

8

9

10

14

15

1

2

3

7

Woodie Fryman reviews all the points we've talked about in pitching with this sequence. Notice especially the perfect "L" angle of the arm in pictures 14 and 15.

12

13

14

4

5

9

10

11

15

16

Tug McGraw of the Philadelphia Phillies demonstrates perfectly the pitching fundamental of burying the pitching shoulder in the ground to ensure getting maximum body power into the pitch. The last four photos really show the perfect balance before launching to the plate. Note the toe of the raised foot pointing toward the ground in photo 2. This will help you keep your shoulders level throughout the delivery. In photo 4, Tug demonstrates the classic position of every great pitcher at this key point in his delivery.

1

2

3

4

5

6

7

8

1

2

3

4

5

Vida Blue bringing it from the left side. Working from the stretch in this sequence, Vida shows a real smooth head fake to first in photos 6 and 7 before picking up his target in photos 8 and 9 and delivering to the plate. Notice the

Sequence continues on next page.

6

classic pitching position in picture 12 that we've talked
about so often in relationship to the perfect form. The
pitching shoulder is buried toward the ground so well in
photos 14 and 15.

10

11

1

16

Check the wind conditions as soon as you arrive at the park. Wind at your back helps your fast ball; wind directly in your face helps your curve.

Don't be "cute" or try to pitch in and out until you are ahead of the batter. Put something on the ball and get it over (you have eight men behind you and even a .300 hitter fails seven out of ten times).

Talk to yourself on the mound; for example, say "low and outside" over and over. This helps shut out all distractions.

When your pitches are coming in higher than you want, aim at the hitter's shoe tops.

Dip the knee of your pivot leg; this gives you a chance to push off as you start your forward motion.

If you are tall, you must dip the knee of your pivot leg to consistently keep the ball low. The dip lowers your projected trajectory and improves the follow-through of your arm and back.

A lazy back leg produces high pitches.

Challenge the hitter with your best pitch, even if it is to the hitter's strength. If a pitcher spot-pitches without his best stuff and makes a mistake, he is in real trouble, but by going with his best stuff he may make a mistake and still get away with it.

Concentration must be total on the mound.

Carl Hubbell once told me that if he came to the mound and asked me for my home phone number and I did not tell him, my concentration was then total, and I had reached the desired point. This is where pressure and second guessing visit the mound to disrupt total concentration. One great pitching coach would rather not visit his pitchers on the mound in most instances, his thinking being that he will partially upset the pitcher's concentration, which must be total.

Do not worry about how tough the hitter is or the last good hit he got off you. Instead, the pitcher should think of the successes he has had against the hitter in similar situations. He has to feel he is the master of the situation.

The result of this thinking will be splendid control, the key to pitching.

4
Developing Your Pitchers

What causes sore arms? How can a coach avoid or minimize them? What is the best way to condition pitchers? How long and how often should a young pitcher throw at the start?

Coaches are always pondering such questions, particularly when organizing preseason practice. The early-spring routine is critical for pitchers. In fact, most baseball men feel that they can minimize or even eliminate arm trouble by breaking in their pitchers' arms properly in the spring.

The writer threw these questions at baseball's premier pitching coach, John Sain, and the wizard of arms came through (as usual) with several splendid ideas on the art of pitching and working with pitchers.

First, Sain feels that every youngster must pitch from his natural throwing angle or he'll eventually end up with arm trouble. There are two ways of determining a boy's natural style.

One is to have him catch some fly balls in the outfield and throw hard to a relay man. As long as the boy doesn't know he's being observed, he'll throw with his natural motion.

The second method is to have the boy work at a pick-up drill (to be explained in Chapter 19) until he becomes tired and then observe how he returns the ball to the thrower, especially with respect to his arm angle and release point. Once the young pitcher's natural motion is determined, that's the way he should pitch to minimize arm trouble.

Knowledgeable coaches are now giving much thought to the arm angle and release point that will produce the most power for the individual pitcher. You can experiment with your pitchers by standing in front of them and clasping their pitching hands at the different release points and angles to see from which point (straight overhand, three-quarters, sidearm, or under-

1

2

3

4

5

6

One of today's outstanding young pitchers is Dennis
Eckersley. Notice in photo 2 how his fingers are hooked
around the baseball. Photo 4 shows you the all-out effort
behind the pitch. Look at the face and neck muscles.

Mel Stottlemyre, the former Yankee ace who was coached by the author, demonstrates a smooth, relaxed, and highly functional delivery. Notice how he steps directly toward the batter, delivers with a fluid but powerful full arm motion, and finishes in perfect fielding position.

Mel Stottlemyre's loose, relaxed grip helps avoid forearm, wrist, and finger tension.

hand) they can deliver the most force against your hand.

Sain makes another point which is often overlooked in young pitchers—arm tension, especially in the reach back. Some boys have a tendency to grip the ball too tightly at the start of the delivery.

A related problem is gripping the ball too hard with the thumb. This destroys the wrist action and helps increase arm tension. Sain suggests that you have the pitcher think he's gripping an egg rather than a baseball. He then won't be so prone to squeeze tightly, especially when taking the ball out of his glove at the beginning of his delivery. He'll thus come to his release point with a relaxed forearm and wrist, which will help him develop a fast arm.

Sain has some highly convincing ideas on how to bring pitchers along in the spring, particularly with respect to the amount and frequency of work. He offers a program which any coach can use, even those who must condition their pitchers in the gym before moving outside.

His method is one of cautious preparation. He uses a stopwatch to make sure of his work schedule; he won't allow a pitcher to throw a minute over the allotted time. That extra pitch or two could be just the ones to strain the arm.

Once a pitcher has gradually worked his arm into condition, he can pitch so hard and long (from two to three hours) that it may become frighteningly stiff. The pain and stiffness will reach such a peak on the second day that the nervous pitcher will begin to think he's had it. The discomfort will subside somewhat on the third day, but not enough for some pitchers to believe that they'll be able to throw the next day. The fourth day brings the "miracle." The arm suddenly feels so loose and strong that the pitcher loses all doubt about going nine innings.

Some words of caution: too much rest can be just as risky as too little rest. Some pitchers, after taking more than their normal rest, become so strong that their pitches tend to straighten out or become so alive as to cause control problems.

Pitchers who develop pains very early in spring training, usually through throwing too hard too early, will tend toward recurrent soreness all season. They may not be able to pitch effectively for months or, sometimes, ever again.

Sain makes sure to prevent his pitcher from throwing too long too early. He has them begin training by warming up slowly for five minutes and then lobbing the ball in batting practice for another five minutes. (He puts a stopwatch on them.) Then the pitchers run sprints, do exercises, and discuss with Sain the mechanics of pitching.

After four days of the five-five program the pitchers are excused from throwing for a day. Then, every other day, they warm up for ten minutes and throw batting practice for another ten. After being on the ten-ten program for two or three days, the hurlers warm up for fifteen minutes, then throw fifteen minutes in a controlled situation, either in the batting cage, gym, or on the mound (if outside). The pitcher, after a day's rest, is now ready to go three or four innings in an exhibition game.

This type of conditioning program will have all the pitchers ready for a complete effort with a strong arm at the opening of the season.

Another major league team offers the following ideas on the conditioning of pitchers:

1. Pickups are beneficial to the arm and the back muscles, especially during spring training.
2. Keep your legs in shape by running.
3. A pitcher must be the best athlete in the club and, therefore, should be in better shape than anyone else.
4. The first ten days are the danger period. In two weeks' time, a pitcher should be able to throw as hard as he likes for two or three innings without any after effects. He should throw every day until he's ready to pitch batting practice and start spinning the ball the first day. (Different muscles come into play in throwing breaking pitches and must be strengthened too.)
5. After a player pitches batting practice (in spring training), send him to the bunting cage (if available) or use him in pick-off plays. This should be done while the pitcher's arm is warm. Never use a pitcher in a throwing drill when his arm is cold. (Don Drysdale spent much time fielding balls placed everywhere in front of the plate and throwing to every base. He felt that this type of practice helped him win one or two games a season.)
6. Keep your pitchers as busy as possible. Let them participate in pepper games if they

1

2

3

4

5

6

Mark "The Bird" Fidrych doing his thing. In photo 3, he has lifted his front knee to help get his throwing arm in position. Even though Mark supposedly has an unorthodox pitching style, notice the perfect balance in photo 4. His pitching fundamentals are perfect. In photo 5, Fidrych demonstrates perfectly the pitching mechanics of bringing the pitching hand back with the palm facing the ground. This allows the hand and wrist to act like a whip. Photos 6 and 7 demonstrate free arm action and burying the shoulder in the ground to get that extra velocity.

7

8

On all balls hit to the left, the pitcher is responsible for covering first base. Although first-baseman Jason Thompson fielded the ball, Vern Ruhle sprinted to the bag as quickly as possible. From this sequence of pictures, can you tell why there are no other base runners?

choose, but don't let them stand around and stiffen up.

To make our pitchers aware of their control, we have our stats man mark every pitch on a pitching chart (actually used by major league clubs). We start out with 30 pitches, 15 from the stretch and 15 from the windup. We then increase it to 40, 60, 80, and so on until we reach 120 pitches, half from the stretch and half from the windup.

After using these charts for a while, you'll find that your pitchers will fall into a definite groove with respect to strikes and balls, and you'll be able to quickly spot potential problems—they show up in the form of sudden changes in the ball-strike ratios. Charting every pitch from the first day of practice can be a real aid in improving a pitcher's concentration and control.

When should a boy actually start throwing breaking pitches? Sain admits this is hard to answer: "It's an individual matter—depending upon the boy's age, build, strength, intelligence, experience, and coordination—and the coach or an experienced baseball man probably will have to make the decision.

"I can tell you this, however: every good curve ball pitcher I know has told me that he started throwing curves at an early age. Most of us started by spinning the ball with extreme caution and with as little strain on the arm as possible, until the muscles were coordinated and strong enough for the actual execution."

Isn't it strange that years ago, before Little League, thousands of kids threw heavily taped baseballs or pitched heavy, waterlogged baseballs for hours without ever injuring their arms!

Most of our preseason conditioning drills for pitchers are done at the end of practice or on days when they aren't working. We run our pitchers about two miles a day for stamina and have them do wind sprints (thirty, from foul line to foul line) for speed. We also have a bench drill wherein the pitcher stands sideways in front of a locker bench and jumps up and down, alternating feet. We begin with a two-minute stint and increase both the time and intensity of the drill as the season progresses. We feel that this helps strengthen the leg muscles used in pitching.

Pickups provide another good drill for the

Jim Lonborg shows perfectly some of the pitching fundamentals we've been discussing. In photo 6, he breaks his hands (glove and ball separate). In the next picture, he lowers the ball as far as possible, allowing his arm to make the longest arc possible for the maximum whip and use of the arm. Notice the cocking of the wrist in photo 8, and in photo 9 you can see perfectly the palm of the pitching hand facing the ground. This provides the maximum whip and use from your wrist, hand, and fingers at the release point in your delivery. In the last picture, Lonborg has gotten everything into the pitch.

2

3

4

6

7

8

9

10

early season. Pitcher A, with two baseballs, faces pitcher B. He rolls one ball after the other about ten feet to B's right and left. B fields the balls and returns them to A, and the drill is repeated. We start with 50 tosses and go up to 150 as the conditioning season progresses.

Weighted baseballs have become quite popular with pitchers today. You may fill a baseball with buckshot or buy a commercial lead baseball weighing between four and five pounds. One of the best exercises is to have the pitcher stand on his toes and reach as high as he can with his weighted ball, as if screwing in a light bulb. A simulated pitch makes another good exercise with the weighted ball. The pitcher goes through his regular motion while holding the ball in his pitching hand and supporting the arm at the elbow with the other hand. This exercise benefits strength, stretching, and flexibility.

Upon moving outdoors, we convert all of our pitchers into infield and outfield fungo hitters. we feel that this hitting action over the course of a season has a positive effect on the shoulders and arms.

Each pitcher keeps a bottle of rubbing compound in his locker. This contains a fifty-fifty mixture of wintergreen and alcohol, which we expect the pitcher to rub vigorously on his entire shoulder and arm area a half hour before pitching, as well as after his post-game shower. With a little food coloring, this is Satchel Paige's "Snake Oil" compound.

The young pitcher with a real herky-jerky motion must be carefully watched. No matter how good he is, he has to abuse his arm and it will be just a matter of time before serious arm trouble crops up. The wise coach will smooth out his motion before this occurs.

5

John Sain on Spinning Pitches

It isn't exactly a secret that the first checkpoint on a pitching prospect is the velocity of his fast ball. With rare exceptions, a youngster must have a strong arm to rate a chance for the majors. Speed is the one quality nobody can teach him. He either has it or he doesn't, though he might slightly improve it with better mechanics.

As important as it is, however, speed isn't the entire answer to pitching success. It's merely the beginning. Few pitchers can get by in fast company with just a fast ball. The prospect must also develop control, a curve ball, and a change of pace. And, in time, as the arm starts losing its elasticity or the batters start catching up with the basic pitches, the smart hurler will develop an "extra" pitch—a slider, sinker, screwball, or some other offbeat pitch.

The moral is fairly obvious: any young pitcher who wants to get anywhere in baseball shouldn't rely on one good pitch, unless he can throw the ball as hard as a Walter Johnson or pitch "butterflies" like Hoyt Wilhelm. The more rounded a pitcher's repertoire, the better his chances for advancement.

I believe the learning process should begin as early as possible; the earlier, in fact, the better. The high school coach might immediately protest: "Do you mean you want me to teach my kids how to throw sliders, sinkers, and knucklers?"

My answer is yes—with reservations. I realize most coaches and physiologists have always discouraged youngsters from fooling around with "freak" deliveries. They believe that the youthful arm isn't strong enough to be "strained" in this fashion, and that it might be permanently injured. They also believe that the boy, at this age, should be concentrating wholly on control of his basic pitches.

I have no quarrel with this reasoning. It is sound, as far as it goes. But I believe this: the earlier a boy starts learning anything, the faster he's going to master it. Why wait until a boy is eighteen or nineteen before teaching him the mechanics of the various types of breaking pitches? You'll be retarding his progress. He's going to need one or more of these pitches in the not-so-distant future, and instead of having them at his command at that time, he's going to have to start learning them.

I don't mean to imply that a 12-, 13-, or 14-year-old boy should be sent out on the mound and taught the curve ball. I do mean that he should be given an understanding of the proper mechanics of all pitches—why rotation is important, how it is applied, what it does to the ball.

How can this be done? For a long time, I used to demonstrate rotation by holding a ball in my left hand and showing the various types of spin with the other. This left something to be desired. The different mechanical actions and rotations were not only difficult to demonstrate,

but could hardly be remembered and much less practiced without abusing the arm.

One afternoon I noticed Ralph Terry on the bench practicing spin by flipping the ball easily in various ways. I said, "Ralph, I'm going to fix up a ball so that you can spin it a whole lot easier and better than that."

Thinking about it on the way home, an idea occurred to me. When I got home, I went into the living room, picked an apple out of the fruit bowl, then plucked the end out of one of the "rabbit ears" (indoor antenna) of my television set. I stuck the thin bar through the apple, and I now had a "baseball" I could spin to my heart's content. The next step was the development of the Baseball Spinner.

With this Spinner and our illustrations, I feel every boy can practice the correct way of spinning a baseball for all types of pitches. I realize that this sort of practice won't guarantee instant success; you won't be able to go out the next day and start snapping off sharp-breaking curves, rising fast balls, and deceptive sinkers. It will, however, provide an understanding of the

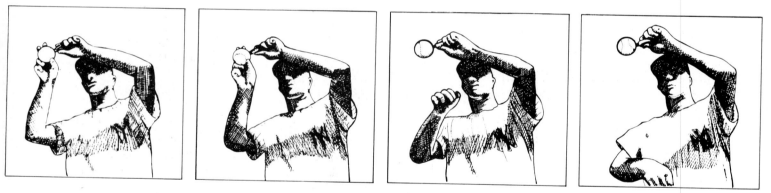

Johnny demonstrates the correct spin for a three-quarter arm fast ball on his unique Baseball Spinner.

After changing the axis of the Baseball Spinner, Sain applies the correct spin for a three-quarter arm curve ball.

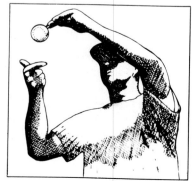

spin you must apply to make the ball do these things.

It's the spin that makes a curve ball curve, a slider slide, a sinker and a screwball sink, and a fast ball rise. And always remember: good breaking stuff must go down.

In the old days, a distinction was made between curves and "drops." The curve was usually a flat, breaking pitch, while the drop did just that. The distinction has long vanished. Since a flat curve isn't usually effective, the good curve ball breaks down. In short, a curve ball, in modern parlance, is a breaking pitch that goes down. The "hanging curve," which is so often stroked out of the park, is merely a curve that hasn't been spun sharply enough to make it drop.

The reason is simple enough. If a curve stays on a horizontal plane, the batter's visual line won't be too badly disconcerted. Even if he's fooled by the pitch, he can continue to bring his bat around on a horizontal plane, pulling it in or reaching out to meet the ball.

When the ball sinks, however, his visual line must suddenly change from the horizontal to the vertical. And if he has been bringing his bat around on a horizontal plane, he'll have to quickly dip it to meet the ball. That takes some doing, particularly if he has already committed himself to a flat swing.

Now let's see how the various spins can be taught with the Baseball Spinner. The handle is held in the non-pitching hand, while the proper spin on the ball is sharply imparted with the pitching hand. The direction in which the handle is pointed is of vital importance, since it puts the baseball in the correct axis for the specific type of delivery and spin.

The grip should be light but firm, not tight, with the two top fingers fairly close together and the thumb directly underneath them. An overly firm grip tightens the muscles on the underside of the forearm, partly locking the wrist. And if there's anything that a good curve-ball pitcher needs, it's a good flexible wrist to get the necessary spin on the ball.

Now, let's proceed to the photos. They show how the Baseball Spinner can be used by both left- and right-handed pitchers in the overhand, three-quarter, and sidearm motions. They dem-onstrate the correct axis for each type of spin, as well as the direction in which the spin should be applied.

FAST BALL

Holding the Spinner in the position shown, apply the spin in the direction indicated by the arrow. This will make the ball rotate back toward you.

It's the speed and spin that makes a fast ball move or hop. The real good overhand fast ball will level off or rise. Both the three-quarter and the sidearm delivery, when thrown with enough speed and spin, will move in on the hitter (right-handed pitcher to right-handed hitter or left-handed pitcher to left-handed batter).

While a fast ball can sometimes be improved through practice and the development of coordination, the best fast balls seem to be rare gifts of nature.

CURVE

Check the direction of the Spinner handle for the proper axis. Place your finger on the ball and then sharply apply spin in the direction of the arrow.

Most pitchers apply this spin by simultaneously pulling down with the fingers and flipping up with the thumb, spinning the ball in the direction of the arrow. The youngster can try spinning the ball with only the top fingers, using a light pull downward in the direction of the arrow. Next, he can try flipping the ball upward, using only the thumb.

The lesson is clear: if he can apply a small amount of spin with each of these methods, the coordination of the two should give him a faster rotation.

After learning to get good rotation on the Spinner, don't immediately start on sharp-breaking curves. After a preliminary warm-up, try throwing about half-speed, applying the spin you've learned on the Spinner. Since you no longer have the ball on a handle, you must now watch the spin while the ball is in flight. In your early attempts, be satisfied if the ball merely

The positions for hands for left-handed
pitchers: curve ball, slider, fast ball, and
sinker.

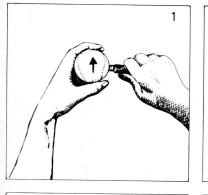

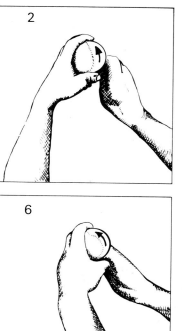

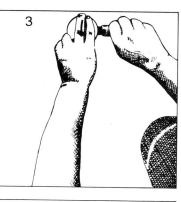

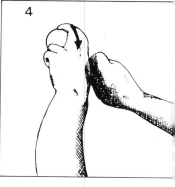

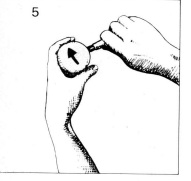

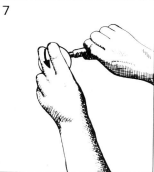

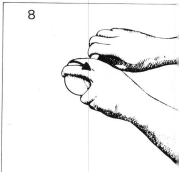

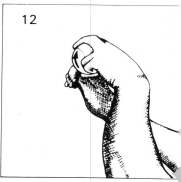

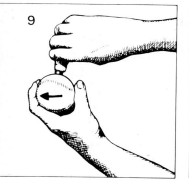

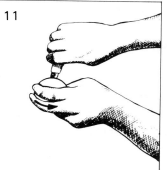

1. Overhand Curve ball
2. Overhand slider
3. Overhand fast ball
4. Three-quarter sinker
5. Three-quarter curve ball
6. Three-quarter slider
7. Three-quarter fast ball
8. Sidearm sinker
9. Sidearm curve ball
10. Sidearm slider
11. Sidearm fast ball
12. Screwball

The positions for hands for right-handed pitchers: curve ball, slider, fast ball, and sinker.

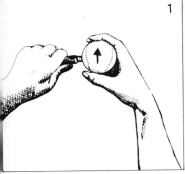

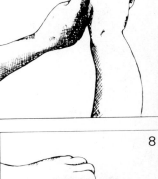

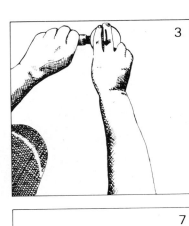

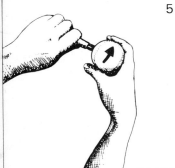

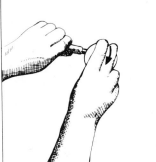

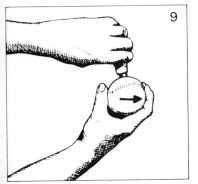

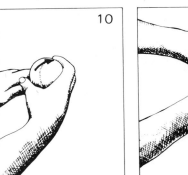

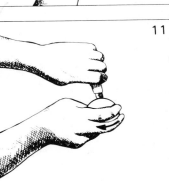

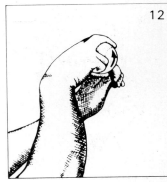

1. Overhand curve ball
2. Overhand slider
3. Overhand fast ball
4. Three-quarter sinker
5. Three-quarter curve ball
6. Three-quarter slider
7. Three-quarter fast ball
8. Sidearm sinker
9. Sidearm curve ball
10. Sidearm slider
11. Sidearm fast ball
12. Screwball

Coach John Sain demonstrates the development of a smooth delivery.

1

5

6

7

11

2

3

4

8

9

1

12

13

Don Gullett illustrates the perfect sequence of pitching from the stretch. Photo 5 shows his perfect balance.

1

2

6

spins in the right direction, even if it doesn't curve.

Before trying to throw faster and sharper breaking curves, make sure you have a smooth delivery and that there's little strain on your arm. As mentioned before, the mechanics should be learned at about half-speed. Most arms are hurt when a pitcher starts losing his temper, showing off, or throwing hard without a proper warm-up.

SLIDER (FAST CURVE)

The slider is really a fast ball with a break at the end. The break may take a little off its speed, but it's a highly effective pitch to go along with the regular fast ball, curve, and change-up.

The axis, or handle, of the Spinner is now pointed downward and to the left side of the plate for a right-handed pitcher, and downward and to the right side of the plate for a left-handed pitcher. Apply the spin by pulling down in the direction of the arrow. This provides an off-center fast ball spin whose axis is downward in the direction of the break.

If this doesn't work, you can experiment with your own ideas. Just remember that most mechanical pitches should be practiced at about half-speed, and that you should wait until you're better coordinated and understand the

mechanics before trying to make a pitch break sharply.

SINKER

Compare the three-quarter sinker and the three-quarter fast ball pictures. You'll notice that the axis in the sinker is downward and slightly forward as the fast ball spin is imparted. Turning the wrist produces a loss of some forward speed, which is why a sinker is slightly slower than a fast ball.

Now compare the sidearm sinker and sidearm

fast ball photos. Again note the axis change and how the fast ball spin is applied in both instances.

SCREWBALL

This is a very difficult pitch to learn and maintain with consistency. It is produced by a combination of spin, change of speed, and motion. The ball acts like a reverse curve, moving out and down when delivered by a left-handed pitcher to a right-handed batter, or by a right-handed pitcher to a left-handed batter. To be effective with this pitch, you must properly coordinate the three aforementioned factors.

Compare the three-quarter screwball and the three-quarter fast ball photos. Notice that the axis changes slightly in each, creating a change in the wrist position. Since the wrist and forearm are sharply turned in—an unnatural action—most people believe the screwball puts a lot of strain on the arm. This strain can be reduced by proper mechanics and a proper delivery.

This applies to all mechanical pitches, plus the fast ball. If the pitcher is unable to realize when he's abusing his arm, a coach or some other knowledgeable baseball man must help supervise his throwing.

When should a boy actually start throwing breaking pitches? I've often been asked this question and I admit it's hard to answer. It's such an individual matter—depending upon the boy's age, build, strength, intelligence, experience, and coordination—that the coach, an experienced baseball man, or perhaps even the boy himself will ultimately make the decision.

I can tell you this, however: every good curve ball pitcher I know has told me he started throwing curves at an early age. Most of us started by spinning the ball with extreme caution, putting as little strain on the arm as possible until the muscles were coordinated and strong enough for the actual execution.

The "secret" lies in careful planning: (1) give the boy a thorough understanding of the mechanics, (2) start him slowly, having him merely spin the ball at half-speed, (3) see that he warms up properly before attempting any hard throws, (4) make sure he has the coordination and strength to attempt these pitches, (5) supervise him carefully to see that he doesn't abuse his

arm. And always remember this about the final point: a boy can hurt his arm throwing fast balls just as easily as he can throwing curve balls.

FIRST THINGS FIRST: DEVELOP A SMOOTH DELIVERY

With nobody on base, take a stance squarely facing the batter. Place the front spike over the edge of the rubber, slightly angled to the right to facilitate the pivot. Set the other foot a few inches back of the rubber. Keep the body fairly erect, with the weight forward and the shoulders level. When taking the sign, hide the ball from the batter. You may place it behind the thigh of the pitching foot. A short windup—one or at most two pumps—loosens the arm and helps bring the weight behind the pitch. Swing the arms up past the hips and join them overhead, making sure to keep the back of the glove turned toward the hitter, thus concealing the ball.

Now the pivot begins. Slide the pitching (front) foot diagonally forward into the hole and turn your body to the right. Then, as the arm goes back, swing the left leg up and around so that you face the batter over the left shoulder. Don't kick the left leg too high; it may throw you off-balance. As you can see, you're now in a perfectly balanced position; in fact, at this point you should be able to come to a stop without falling either forward or backward. Just before bringing the pitching arm forward, start the forward stride with the left leg. Hit the ground with it flat, not on the heel, and point the toes directly at the plate. The arm is brought through in a free, easy, but powerful motion with the weight flowing from the rear to the front foot, the unwinding of the hips providing both momentum and power.

Don't stop jerkily after the ball leaves the hand. Bend the back and let the arm relax as soon as the ball is released, thus relieving the tension on the entire arm. As the arm follows through to the opposite side, the right leg comes forward into a squared-off position and the glove is brought around to the front of the body. You're now in perfect fielding position, ready to move right, left, or forward with equal facility. Now check the head. Note how it remains fixed from the start to the finish of the delivery.

6

John Sain on Pitching

After a brilliant career with the Braves and the Yankees, tall, quiet, gentlemanly John Sain moved his gear into another part of the locker room and launched another dazzling career, this time as a pitching coach. First with the Yankees, then with the Twins, Tigers, White Sox, and now with the Atlanta Braves, the Arkansas traveler has established himself as the nonpareil of pitching coaches. Jim Brosnan, an outstanding pitcher before he turned writer, has said that Sain's approach may have done as much for pitching in the 1960s as the lively ball did for batting in the late 1920s and the 1930s.

Nobody has ever known more about pitching than John Sain. Nobody has ever been able to articulate or teach it as well. And probably nobody in baseball has ever been more candid about his knowledge and more willing to reveal everything he knows. The result has been a bonanza for everyone who has ever talked pitching with him.

The writer presented himself to Sain and received the typical Sain hospitality—several hours of fabulous pitching talk! Some of the highlights of this conversation, in question-and-answer form, follow.

How would you go about developing a young pitcher?

I'd first determine the boy's natural way of throwing. One way of doing this is by hitting fungoes to him in the outfield and watching him throw the ball back. That generally will be his natural way of throwing and the way he should pitch.

I'd then try to develop his pitching motion—a simple, smooth, free, and rhythmical delivery. Coaches who disregard these basic mechanics

Notice how both Dave McNally and Nolan Ryan have their arms in a perfect position to throw and how everything becomes a quick downward motion. Have someone in your family or your coach take a picture of you; if you are not in this position at your release point, your pitching mechanics are basically wrong.

and principles of pitching form and let the boy abuse his arm will wind up with ineffective and sore-armed pitchers.

What do you stress in a smooth motion?

I want the pitcher to put his hip pocket into the hitter's face. This is especially important for the sidearm pitcher. Although the overhand and the three-quarter pitchers also must emphasize this point, it is not as imperative.

This sort of pivot or turn allows the arm to keep up with and work with the body. If this isn't stressed, the pitcher's body can be too quick for his arm, thus destroying his rhythm and power, as his arm will have to hurry to catch up with his body.

What are the pitcher's chief tools?

Velocity, rotation, change of speed, and deception with control. At the same time, pitching must be simplified. The coach should always be thinking of how to make everything simpler.

Rotation can be practiced anywhere off the field with the John Sain Spinner (see Chapter 5). This device enables a coach to show any young pitcher the proper spin from any pitching angle.

How important is spin?

It's the spin that makes a curve ball curve; a slider slide; a sinker and a screwball sink; and a fast ball rise. And remember—good breaking stuff always must go down.

The reason is simple. If a curve stays on a horizontal plane, the batter's line of vision won't be too badly disconcerted. Even if he's fooled by a pitch, he can continue to bring his bat around on a horizontal plane—pulling it in or reaching out—to meet the ball.

When the ball sinks, however, his visual line must suddenly change from the horizontal to the vertical. And if he has been bringing his bat around on a horizontal plane, he'll now have to quickly dip it to meet the ball. This takes some doing, particularly if he has already committed himself to a flat swing.

Mel Stottlemyre puts it all together.

1

2

3

4

5

6

7

8

9

In this sequence Vern Ruhle illustrates the smooth, balanced delivery which is a key to good control. Notice in photo 7 how the body and arm are together perfectly at the release point. In photo 8, you can see how the pitching shoulder is "buried" in the ground. Study this excellent sequence and see how the rhythm and timing are merged for maximum use.

1

2

3

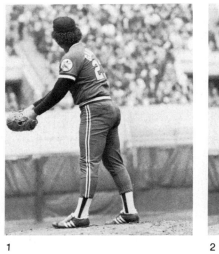

4

5

6

7

8

9

10   11   12

13   14

Wayne Garland pitching from the stretch—a fine sinker-ball pitcher with excellent form. He finishes up in splendid fielding position. Notice in photos 1, 2, and 3 how he stretches and gets himself set in a relaxed position. In photos 6, 7, and 8, you can see how Garland bends his back knee and really launches his body from the rubber. In the last photos, you can see the excellent pitching form. In photo 13, Wayne is in perfect fielding position.

1

2

3

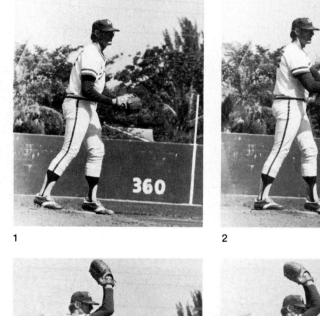

4

5

6

7

8

9

10

11

12

13

14

15

Paul Splittorf shows his outstanding pitching fundamentals from the left side. (Port-siders always seem to have classic pitching form.) Paul is loose in his preliminary wind-up with his arms free, the ball well hidden. Notice in photo 8 a real key teaching point: if you are a tall pitcher, keep the ball low. You must bend your back leg at the knee, which allows you to lower your body and drive off the pitching rubber (much as a plane shooting off a catapult on an aircraft carrier). In photos 10 and 11, he has the toe of his front foot pointing down to help keep his shoulders level. Also note that he's kept his front shoulder closed. In the last two pictures, Splittorf is really burying that pitching shoulder in the ground.

1

2

3

4

5

6

7

8

9

Al Hrabosky demonstrates his all-out pitching delivery which has made him one of the top relievers in recent years. In the last three photos, his total use of his body is apparent, which helps him get that little extra on the pitch. This will help it to move. In the first picture, note how relaxed the wrist and fingers are so that he will get maximum whip and snap from them. (Al is not trying to squeeze the juice out of the ball.) Photo 2 is a classic for young pitchers, an excellent illustration of hiding the ball. You can't even see the top of his wrist with a telephoto lens. In photo 5, we see demonstrated all the pitching fundamentals we have been talking about. Notice Hrabosky's total concentration; his *head* and *eyes* are glued on his target in each step of his delivery.

1

2

3

4

5

Bert Blyleven, one of the best curve-ball pitchers in the game today, shows his splendid form. In photo 4, notice how his fingers are hooked around the ball for maximum spin. His thumb is tucked to be able to flip the ball out and give it extra spin at the last second. Also see how the narrow part of his arm is going to be facing the hitter as he releases this curve ball.

What kind of grip do you advocate for the curve ball?

The grip should be light but firm, not tight, with the two top fingers fairly close together and the thumb directly underneath them. An overly firm grip tightens the muscles on the underside of the forearm, partly locking the wrist. And if there's anything that a good curve-ball pitcher needs, it's a good flexible wrist to get the necessary spin on the ball.

Your fast curve, or slider, has revolutionized pitching. How do you teach it?

The fingers are moved slightly to the right of the fast-ball grip, and the fingers are pulled over and straight down on the ball. The elbow is slightly bent and closer to the body and head. The smooth delivery and good follow-through place hardly any strain on the elbow.

The thumb doesn't grip too tightly, as this can spoil the wrist action. In fact, the thumb can sometimes be flipped from underneath the ball to provide even more spin.

The faster the rotation, the sharper the drop. The motion is so easy and the strain so little that Whitey Ford started throwing this pitch from almost the first moment he tried it.

The fast curve is really a fast ball with a break at the end. The break may take a little off its speed, but it's a highly effective pitch to go along with the regular fast ball, curve, and changeup.

What is your theory on the release of the ball?

You must have a quick forearm and wrist action. The White Sox pitchers did this real well. I like to have the pitcher think curve ball on every pitch until just before the release.

If it's a curve ball he's throwing, he just thinks curve ball all the way through. If it's going to be a fast curve, he thinks curve ball until just before the release and then thinks fast ball the rest of the way. Quite obviously he must have command of all his pitches.

What do you do with the pitcher who seems to have lost his stuff for no apparent reason?

A pitcher will lose a pitch when he begins neglecting it. If he has three or four pitches, it would be wise for him to spend fifty percent of his time on his best pitch.

How do you go about teaching pitchers to work on the hitters?

I don't feel that you can teach each pitcher a different way to pitch to the hitters. Basically, the pitcher should work to his power, which usually is from the waist down. And he should put his best stuff on the ball. If he then makes a mistake high, he may get away with it. If he's just pitching to spots, however, he'll be in real trouble if he misses.

What are your thoughts on working from the stretch position?

In holding a man on first, it's important to have the knees bent. If you keep them straight and then bend them in the delivery, you'll be giving the runner a good tip-off.

It is also essential, of course, to develop quickness to the plate, and you'll have to experiment until you arrive at the best way to do this. As a pitcher, I closed my stance by moving my front leg over toward third.

With a man on third and the steal or the squeeze a distinct possibility, the pitcher should work from a stretch. Being able to see the runner (if he's right-handed), he can take his time and put something on the ball. When pitching from his regular stance, he'll be inclined to hurry his pitch for fear of the runner taking off on him.

What are the important mental aspects of pitching?

I like a pitcher who, after losing, doesn't blame it on the breaks, but goes on trying to find ways to improve himself. The pitcher must always stay loose, particularly in a jam.

How many times have you seen a pitcher in a tight spot make up his mind to blow the ball by the hitter? Just before the release, he'll really muscle up and then let go. The result is an unnatural delivery with a poor wrist action that puts less, rather than more, on the ball.

A smart catcher can be a big psychological help to the pitcher. The catcher who really knows how to handle pitchers will come out to the mound and ask "What's your plan? What do you want to throw?" or possibly "What are you trying to do?"

This kind of catcher is giving the pitcher credit for having some sense and thus builds his confidence. It takes a special temperament to pitch. The two people who really look bad whenever they show emotion on the field are the pitcher and the manager.

Concentration is another big item—it must be total. This is where pressure and second guessing visit the mound. Also the worry about how tough the particular hitter is or about the last good hit he got off you.

The pitcher must think positively. Instead of thinking about the hits, he should think of the success that he's had against the hitter or against other hitters in similar situations. And anytime he gets the hitter out on a line drive, he shouldn't think of it as luck. He should think of it as a good pitch. He must feel that he's the master of the situation.

About how often should a pitcher throw?

Contrary to some theories, I want him to throw some every day—enough to get loose but not enough to abuse his arm. You must develop your pitcher's arm and one of the best ways of doing this is by having him throw. I feel that the typical pitcher is ready, mentally, to pitch every third day, though I realize that, physically, this schedule would be difficult to maintain over a season.

We often hear the term that so and so is a five- or six-inning pitcher. What are your thoughts on this?

It's possible that the pitcher simply lacks stamina, that he fatigues easily. The more likely cause, however, is that the pitcher hasn't enough equipment; the batters begin catching up with him after five or six innings. What he needs, as a rule, is another pitch.

What use do you make of pitching charts?

We can discern several things from a good chart. Generally, a batter will hit his ground balls and pop outs in one direction and his line drives in another. And it's a big help to know which pitches he hits where. Also, if the pitcher feels he's getting killed with one of his pitches, we can go to the charts and see what's happening with that pitch.

The pitching chart in Chapter 23 shows the type of chart we use. We use red for base hits and blue or green for fly outs and ground balls.

What do you try to do in coaching and working with pitchers?

First, I like to put myself in the pitcher's shoes. I say to myself: "How would I pitch with this man's style and stuff?" Then I suggest two or three ideas which might help him. Most of the time he'll try them out and find the one which helps him most. Once he's satisfied that it can help him, he'll adopt it and work on it.

If I tried to force him to throw one way, he'd probably resist me. This is the one flaw of many otherwise fine pitching coaches—they try to make all pitchers throw the way they did, even though their physiques and tools are completely different.

How should a pitcher get ready for spring training, especially in a winter climate?

The two drills I particularly like for this purpose are bench jumping and cement-block drill. In the first drill, the pitcher jumps up and down on a bench or chair (whose surface is about three feet off the floor) fifty times. Later, he can increase the repetitions and do it with both legs. This not only builds up the legs but simulates the pitcher's leg kick.

The cement-block drill can be used in a basement, gym, or any other area. After obtaining or making up a solid three-foot square cement block, you should smooth one side so that it won't scuff your baseballs and paint the strike zone on it. You should then run two pipes from the top down to the floor.

You can then either pitch to the painted target, working on your different pitches (particularly the low strike), or you can set up the block as first, second, or third base and work on your pick-off moves. These two aids really helped me in preparing for the season.

7

Catching

FUNDAMENTALS OF CATCHING:

Catcher Should Remind Pitcher:

1. When fielding bunts, where to throw.
2. When starting double play, who's covering second.
3. Balls hit to left side; break toward first.
4. Back up third and home plate when throws coming to those bases.
5. The score; the number and importance of outs.

Catcher Should Remind Third Baseman:

1. Speed of runner.
2. Bunts, when in order.
3. To be cut-off man on single to left when man on second.
4. Going for double play and letting one run score.
5. Amount of room third baseman has when going for any pop fly.
6. Give inside target to third baseman when man is scoring so that third baseman will not hit runner.

Catcher Should Remind First Baseman:

1. Speed of runner.
2. When bunt in order.
3. When base runners may be stealing.
4. When to be cut-off man and where to be standing.
5. Importance of tying and winning runs.
6. Amount of room any first baseman may have when going for pop flies.

Catcher Should Remind Pitcher:

1. Pick up target.
2. Concentrate.
3. Use some deception in motion, etc.
4. Pitch low.
5. Follow through and bend back.
6. Shove off back leg and drive toward home plate.
7. What bases to cover.
8. Change speeds.
9. Don't be a thrower.
10. Think about what he is doing.
11. When to cover first base and back up other bases.

In the first few photos, Carlton Fisk is thinking of what pitch he wants to throw to Rico Carty. One of the fine right-handed power hitters in the game, he is using multiple signs in photos 4–8. Notice how close Fisk works to the hitter and the splendid low target he gives for a big catcher. In photo 12, his arms are outside of his legs for quick movement. By doing this, a catcher will not tie himself up.

1

2

3

7

8

9

Giving Signs:
Squat Position—Right Knee at Pitcher.
Right Wrist Close to Groin.
Glove Hand Extends over Left Knee with
Pocket Facing Plate.

1. Position of glove, blocking vision of coaches.
2. Holding of glove same position whether fast ball or curve.
3. *Think of situation, what needed, ground ball, etc.*
4. *When in tough spot, use pitcher's best pitch.*
5. *Don't be afraid to pitch out when you think runner may be going or when you want to attempt to pick someone off.*

6. *Don't give signs in too big of hurry—think out situation.*
7. Don't give signs too low so that on-deck hitter can see them below his bottom or between your legs.

After Giving Sign, Don't:

1. Become a jumping jack and jump up in front of umpire. Stay low.
2. Snap or jab at ball. Receive the ball gracefully—let the ball come to you.
3. Bring ball into strike zone.
4. Move up on curve ball.
5. Move back on fast ball. (Stay in same position.)

4

5

6

10

11

12

After Giving Sign, You Now Become a Receiver:

1. Stay low.
2. Don't have your tail way up in the air.
3. Don't have your tail dragging on the ground.
4. Spread your legs.
5. Bend arms slightly in a relaxed fashion.
6. Open up arms and have palms up.
7. Left foot up in front slightly.
8. Point toes out.
9. Stay on balls of your feet.
10. Keep elbows out from in between legs; this allows for freedom and quickness of movement.
11. *Keep arms out for freedom.*

With Runners on Base:

1. Expect every runner to be a base stealer.
2. Be alert and catch all thrown balls. Don't let anything get by, especially with men on base.
3. *Think,* anticipate when the steal may be in order.
4. *Put weight on left foot, then weight to back foot* (helps you throw).
5. Create rhythm when catching ball; bring glove and hand back together, swaying shoulders.
6. Take ball out of glove as glove and hand come back, cock wrist, and throw from over the top.
7. Grip ball across seams for accuracy.
8. Keep bottom hand horizontal to the ground, down just slightly.
9. Don't be afraid to pitch out.
10. Don't be afraid to try and pick a runner off. This will depend on score, outs, etc.
11. Assume stance as close to batter as possible.
12. Don't take too many steps when releasing ball—it is more of a pivot than a step. (Think of a barber pole running through the middle of your body.)

Shifting When Runners Going:

1. Pitch to right, step with right foot.
2. Pitch to left, step with right foot; this will get your catcher moving toward second and cut the throwing distance down.

3. When step is to the left and throw is necessary, bring left foot behind right.
4. Anticipate the shifting more so when calling for breaking pitches.
5. Use the left foot as a guide, and step toward the base you are throwing to.

All Catchers Should:

1. Block balls in dirt by falling to knees.
2. Keep runners close to bases by attempting pick offs.
3. Field ground balls and taps in front of plate by using two hands. Use glove as scoop and bring hand into glove.
4. *Throw bat out of way when play is coming into home plate.*

Catching Drills for Improvement:

1. Keep equipment on during most drills for agility purposes.
2. *Two catchers throw low balls in dirt to each other, sixty feet (drop to knees to block ball).*
3. Two catchers throw balls on short hop to each other, 100 feet (relax arms). Let ball come to you.
4. Throw in squatting position to second base; repetition will be necessary.
5. Make imaginary tags in front of home plate with all balls thrown home during infield practice.

1

2

Duane Kuiper gets to the bag early and in perfect position to take the throw from the catcher. Then, as the ball arrives, he goes down low and with a smooth motion tags the runner and gets his glove out of there. Notice in photos 5 and 6 how he gives with his arm in the direction the runner is sliding. A perfect tag.

3

4

6

7

6. Field topped balls out in front of home plate using glove as scoop.

7. Step with front foot to bag you are throwing to at all times.

8. *Bring both glove and arm back with rhythm when throwing.*

9. Get in the habit of throwing with fingers across seams; set ball in glove.

10. Stay behind home plate when throwing in infield practice.

11. *Throw at extended distances to strengthen arm.*

12. Practice catching pop flies. (Remember to throw mask off and out of way.)

13. *Make certain palms up. All pop flies out in front of home plate will come down like right-hander's curve ball and will go away. Turn around and let the ball come into your chest.*

14. *Go to fence and screen areas, then come away to catch pop-ups; ball will come back.*

15. Field balls in foul territory, and make throws to first and third bases.

16. Imaginary first and third situation, looking runner back at third, then throw through, throwing ball back to pitcher (hard), throwing to third base.

17. Stance is important. Practice staying on balls of feet, feet open, pointing out, and left leg and foot up in front of right leg.

18. Practice receiving ball; let ball come to you, don't jab.

19. Bring ball into strike zone when warming pitchers up; this will get you into habit when game starts.

20. Make pitcher work when warming him up. Remember, you are preparing him for game, not just playing catch.

21. Catching batting practice is an important drill—use it wisely—don't be lazy.

22. *The most important drill of all is to train yourself to think . . . think . . . think . . . think . . . think.*

1

5

6

Duane Kuiper shows perfect form on fielding a ground ball, getting low in photos 1 and 2 and coming up with the ball in photo 3 as it takes a high hop. Notice how both hands are close together in photo 3 to receive the ball softly. He is in good balance before he throws, and then lets the arm follow through in photo 9.

2

3

4

7

8

9

8

Basic Defensive Play

A great many baseball games are given away by the defense. Try to cut down on losing games this way.

Infield Play

Try to develop leaders and players who will take charge of their own individual positions. Stress with every infielder that he should:

1. Know what to do with the ball before it is hit to him.
2. *Practice moving on the pitch, have a slight movement as the ball approaches the plate. Don't be a flatfooted infielder.*
3. Be sure infield drills cover every possible play for that position.
4. Determine the speed at which a ball is hit.

This will help him to determine which base to throw it to.
5. Know the outs and innings.
6. Try to determine upon going left or right which base will be the easiest to make a play at.
7. Warming-up. Throw from longer distances. This will stretch out arms for repeat plays as well as strengthen the arm.
8. Use pepper practice for bettering agility and quickness of hands. Try not to use more than three players and spread them out.
9. Know the pitch for advantages of shading hitter a specific way. Use word sign with infielders to prepare them. Shortstop tells third baseman, second baseman tells first baseman . . .
10. Go back for all pop flies until outfielder runs you off. The pop fly is yours until you hear him; then get out of the way. (Some-

Right: Willie Randolph illustrates Bud Harrelson's idea of showing the button on his cap to the coach. Rich Rollins' idea of moving as the ball is being pitched is illustrated by Willie in photos 1 and 2. You can't be flat-footed and be a good infielder. Photo 5 shows perfect form to field the ball; notice the glove flat on the ground, knees bent, hands out in front—the perfect position. Photos 7, 8, and 9 show the shuffle, cross-hop, and the throw to nail the runner.

1   2   3

5   6

4

7

8

9

times the infielder must dive flat out on ground.)

11. Run catchers off most pop flies. It is a much easier play for the infielder coming in to make, especially since the infielder doesn't have gear on, as the catcher does.

12. When the double play is in order, be sure of getting the lead runner.

   a.) On the double play infielder catching ground ball, second man on other end of double play is man who executes it.

   b.) Make sure the infielder gives the executor a good throw, and don't hide the ball.

   c.) *Make certain ground ball hit is really a double play ball. Many double plays are mishandled because speed of ball was really not fast enough for double play to* be completed in the first place.

13. *Teach each infielder to know the range of the infielder playing next to him.*

14. *Know the arm strength of the outfielders. This will determine how far out the infielder must go when acting as cut-off man.*

15. *Gauge the running speed of the hitter.*

16. *Make sure that the infielder sees all opposing base runners tag the base.*

17. Stay with the ball. Should the infielder boot it, there is always the chance of coming up with the ball the second time and throwing the runner out. In retrieving ground balls, be very quick and alert; above all, do not get excited.

18. Even the greatest of infielders constantly practice handling all types of ground balls to keep themselves on the beam in this

Total effort in making a put-out.

important phase of infield play.

a.) Brooks Robinson used to come out and sometimes spend as much as thirty minutes several hours before a game having a coach fungo all types of ground balls and line drives at him.

b.) When your infielders become very adept at fielding ground balls, you may put hundreds of rubber bands on the barrel end of one fungo bat. This will make every ball you hit come off the bat with different English on it and make each ground ball a different adventure.

c.) Practice getting the jump on the ball in batting practice off the bat. The ball reacts the closest to game conditions in this type of practice.

19. When a hitter is drag bunting, infielders should watch the barrel of the bat for a tip-off.

20. Play the ball, never let the ball play you.

a.) Get to line of ball fast; then change speeds and judge trying to catch the ball at the top of the hop.

b.) If in between hops, charge the ball and try to trap it on the short hop.

21. When a ball is nine inches or more off your right foot, turn glove hand over and backhand the ball. This keeps glove hand relaxed and easy to move quickly.

22. With man on second and two outs, infielder should always strive to knock the ball down to save a run, holding the man on third.

23. *All* pop flies directly behind the first and third basemen will be the responsibility of the second baseman and the shortstop.

9

Infield Play: The Fundamentals for Proper Fielding

1. Foot spread depends upon most comfortable position for individual infielder. Not too wide. One foot slightly in front of the other.
2. Toes should be pointed out.
3. Keep weight on balls of feet.
4. Knees slightly bent.
5. Body leaning forward.
6. Hands off knees.
7. Body in semi-crouch.
8. As pitcher releases ball, *a slight movement to get body going.* Shuffle.
9. Lay glove open as you come into ball.
10. Do not wait until last second to open glove. This will cause flipping action.
11. Center the ball in the middle of your body.
12. Try to get in front of every ball. When not possible, don't be afraid to backhand the ball.
13. Keep your tail low at all times.
14. Lay glove on the ground—let ball roll into it.
15. Keep your head down and watch the ball go into glove.
16. Keep off your heels and go to ball.
17. Charge everything you can.
18. Have relaxed hands. Do not jab or be stiff with glove. Relax; don't be a cement hands.
19. On ball hit to infielder's throwing side, make sure back leg and foot are thrown out and shoved along top of dirt with sliding type action. When fielder about to catch ball, then plant back leg.
20. Infielder must establish in his mind his weak and strong side. He then must lean toward side he doesn't go well to until this is improved.
21. Infielder should not play too deep or too

Flynn takes a short shuffle in photo 1 after fielding the ball and keeps himself in perfect balance. Notice in photo 3 the full extension of his arm in throwing. Head and eyes are on his throwing target (first base throughout). Note in photo 2 that he does not take a long wind-up in cocking his arm.

1

2

3

4

5

shallow. Cut down the angle as best he can. This can be determined by coach's evaluation of his own arm and range.

22. It is most times easier to go to glove side.
23. A crossover step should be used when a lateral movement is necessary.
24. When fielding ground ball, keep hands out in front of body. Don't field ball with hands close in.
25. On bad hops, the infielder should act rather than react; never let the ball play you.
26. Catch the ball when it is to your advantage.
    a.) The height of the hop.
    b.) The short hop.
    c.) The long, in-between hop.
27. Keep hands below the ball.
28. Remember, a ball will come up more than it will down—stay low.
29. *Get as many ground balls as possible. This is where infielders are made, at the other end of a fungo stick.*

TIPS ON THROWING

1. Accuracy is the most important part of throwing.
2. Repetitious throwing will develop accuracy.
3. Every time a ball is thrown between two people, a spot should be picked out, and the players should throw to it.
4. Don't just throw for the sake of warming up. Throw for improved accuracy.
5. For accuracy and better carry, get in the habit of throwing from over the top.
6. When possible, set fingers across the seams.
7. Infielders, outfielders, and catchers should follow through with their throws just as pitchers. Bring your arm through.
8. All plays in the infield cannot be made from coming over the top. At times, the infielder as well as catcher may have to come from the side for execution. Be smart enough to know when this is necessary.
9. Throw at over-extended distances to develop arm strength.
10. The charging of a ground ball will help to get off a better and harder throw.
11. Infielders, outfielders, and catchers forget about warming up with knuckle and curve balls.

TIPS FOR TAGGING RUNNERS

1. Time permitting, try to straddle the bag and receive throw at point directly above the bag.
    a.) The ball can travel faster to that point than the reaching fielder's hands can bring the ball back.
2. Make all tags with back of glove hand.
    a.) Hand remains relaxed and moves quickly.
    b.) Runner will have less of a chance of kicking the ball out of your glove.
3. Get in the habit of being a quick, aggressive tagger, and never leave glove hand down when possible.
4. Make certain the umpire has called the play before tossing the ball to a fellow player.
5. Runner must come to the bag, so do not reach out to make the tag. By reaching out, a trick slide will evade the tag.
6. Be alert for the over-sliding of runners if the tag has been missed.
7. After making a tag, be ready to throw to another base for a continuing play.

INFIELD DRILLS FOR IMPROVEMENT

1. Get as many ground balls hit to you as possible.
2. Use infield practice as a tool to make you better. It's not just something to do before the game starts.
3. Play in pepper games as much as possible, two to a game.
4. *In pepper games, use one hand.*
5. *Skip rope for agility and quickness.*
6. *Get body moving to improve range.*
7. *Spread out and do long pickups with other infielder, throwing ground balls to left and right, underhanded, planting the back leg whenever possible.*
8. *Put light weights on ankles for a short period when fielding ground balls.*
9. Practice double play over and over.
10. Throw at extended distance to lengthen out arm and improve strength.
11. Pick out a spot and throw to it when playing catch with other infielder.
12. Third baseman, get a slow thrown ball to him on side lines just as if topped ball.

1

In photo 1, infielder gets glove closed and makes tag with the back of the glove facing the runner. Notice then how he gets the glove hand out of there quickly.

Come in and pick this ball up in a semi-arc; pick it up barehanded. *Grab down on ball just as if you were going to shove it in ground.*

13. Practice the crossover step even when not fielding ball. Make imaginary ball to both right and left.
14. Throw ball underhanded with other infielder. Stiff wrist, just as if double play being made. This can be done on side lines as well as during infield practice.
15. When playing catch or playing pepper, let your hands relax. Get the feeling of ball coming into your hands softly. . . . Don't jab or be stiff.
16. Shortstop or second baseman should not get too big a glove. Use a glove that you can handle, not one that is difficult to get ball out of.
17. Catch as many pop flies as possible.
18. Practice going back on ball. Really push yourself to be in position to field ball with back to outfield.
19. Practice going to weak side.

3

4

10
Shortstop and Second Base Combination

The shortstop is the most important infielder of them all. His application is somewhat different, as he is the key to the double play, defense against the double steal, cut-offs, etc. The shortstop should:

1. Anticipate at all times what he is going to do with ball before it is hit to him.
2. Stay on top with most throws.
3. On ball hit to his right, throw right leg and slide along top of dirt as going to ball. As ball is fielded, plant foot and throw against it.
4. Not play too deep when double play is in order. Cut down the angle by coming in. Cheat toward bag when double play is in order.
5. Establish in own mind his weak and strong side. Cheat toward the weak side.
6. Cross over more than any other infielder because of greater area to cover.

7. Verbally keep second baseman, third baseman, and pitcher alive.
8. Charge ball more than any other infielder.
9. Cover second base when bunt is in order.
10. Hold runners close. Don't let them get big leads.
11. Let second baseman cover second base when double steal is being made, unless a left-handed pull hitter is hitting. Then shortstop takes bag. When second baseman is taking bag, advise him verbally when runner on third base is breaking for home so that he can come up from bag to make play.

IN MAKING THE DOUBLE PLAY, THE SHORTSTOP SHOULD

1. Not feel every ball hit with a man on is a

double-play ball. Speed of ball, where ball is hit, will determine this.

2. Always get the lead man. Let the second baseman execute the double play; shortstop catches the ball.

3. Let pitcher know who is covering second with man on first.

4. Cover second base on all balls hit back to pitcher, unless a real dead right-handed pull hitter. Then second baseman takes bag.

5. Charge the bag hard. Then, slow down with a slight shuffle to determine in what direction throw is coming.

6. Step with left foot, then tag the bag with right foot. This can be a tag or a drag. The ball thrown on the outside: tag bag with right foot and shove off hard out of an oncoming runner's way. Ball thrown on the inside: tag bag with left foot, shove off, plant right leg, and throw. When shortstop takes play by himself, tag bag with left leg, stay behind bag, tag the bag while making the throw.

7. Throw the ball low, make the runner get down.

8. Should either the shortstop or second baseman have a real weak arm, the man with the strongest arm should cover on balls hit back to the pitcher and in double play situation.

9. Have an understanding with second baseman as to who is covering bag. Do this by hiding mouth with glove. Closed mouth will mean (me), open mouth will mean (you).

10. Determine, based upon distance from bag, if a throw is necessary or if an underhand toss will get the runner.

11. When using the underhand toss, give it to second baseman firm. Stiff wrist will help accuracy.

12. Tag the bag by self. When not necessary, don't handle the ball twice. (Stay behind bag when making tag. As planting left foot down and making contact, release ball.)

13. Draw a line in infield practice. Balls on one side of line will be tossed; other side must be thrown. When game time comes, it will be fixed in player's mind what to do naturally.

14. Don't hide throws from the second baseman; let him see the ball at all times.

In this sequence, the shortstop is executing the twin killing with real polish. He has gotten the feed in plenty of time. Notice in photo 1 that he has both hands together for a quick release. He then shuffles across the bag and makes a powerful throw. In photo 4, he takes a hop with both feet after throwing the ball. This takes the weight off his feet and legs and helps prevent an injury when he falls. In photo 2, the shortstop drops his arm down. This ensures that the runner will hit the dirt and slide early.

4

15. If ball is booted, stay at bag. Act as first baseman would.

Shortstop—Second Baseman—Cut-Offs and Relays:
Balls in left field and left center area, shortstop relay man. Balls in right field and right center area, second baseman relay man.

1. Get in position as soon as possible; hold hands high in U-shape and holler *"Hit me, hit me."* Let outfielder know where you are.

2. Take throws from the outfielder from side position and not with back facing infield.

This will have your hips out of way and make it easier to get off quicker, more accurate throw. Set back foot; however, don't throw off balance.

3. When acting as back-up man, let other infielder know where to throw the ball. A loud verbal command is what is needed. Be alive for poor throw when acting as back-up man.

4. When backing up other infielder, be alive for poor throw; then make play.

5. The depth of how far out you go is determined by the strength of your arm and the strength of the outfielder's arm.

6. When third baseman acting as cut-off man,

shortstop covers third base.

7. When lining up throw from outfield, glance back to see you have positioned yourself properly to base you will be throwing to.

8. Go back on all pop flies until outfielder runs you off. Also, make an effort to field all pop flies down third base foul line. Again, only until outfielder runs you off.

THE SECOND BASEMAN SHOULD:

1. Knock the ball down at all times, yours is a short throw.

2. *On a hard hit ground ball, no one on, don't be afraid to drop to one knee.*

Shortstop goes into hole and tries to backhand the ball. In photo 1, glove is low and ready for a quick backhand; photo 2, body is stretched as far as possible and low. Hard hit ball went through for a hit.

1   2

3   4

3. Establish the range of the first baseman; run him off most balls to your left.

4. Most times use a three-quarter type throw. When acting as a relay man, however, as well as making throws home, stay up on top for better accuracy as well as carry.

5. Not get in the habit of flipping the ball; arm strength cannot be developed this way.

6. Verbally keep shortstop, first baseman, and pitcher alive.

7. Communicate with shortstop on who is covering bag. Let shortstop determine this by hiding mouth with glove, using closed mouth (me), open mouth (you).

8. Anticipate at all times what he is going to do with ball before it is hit to him.

9. On ball hit to second baseman's right, throw out right leg and slide along top of dirt as going to ball. As ball is fielded, plant right foot and throw against it.

10. Cover first base when bunt is in order.

11. Make every effort to get to pop fly down right field line that first baseman can't get.

12. Go back on all pop flies until outfielders run you off.

13. Don't play too deep; he must cheat on double play as well as covering bag for steals.

14. When covering first base with bunt in order to go to bag, play bag as first baseman would. Don't time it to just barely get there. Be there early to give a target.

15. Cover bag when double steal is in order, unless a real dead left-handed pull hitter is hitting.

16. When covering the bag for defense of the double steal, go directly to bag and listen for the verbal command from the shortstop. If the runner on third base is going for home, second baseman then will have to come up from the bag and make the throw to home. Catch ball on edge of grass. If the runner stays, then lay back and tag runner out coming in.

IN MAKING THE DOUBLE PLAY, THE SECOND BASEMAN SHOULD:

1. Not feel that every ball hit with a man on is a double play ball. Speed of ball, where ball is hit will determine this.

2. Always get the lead man; second baseman's job is first to catch the ball, then give shortstop a good throw. *The shortstop will execute the double play.*

3. Shortstop will cover all balls hit back to pitcher unless a real dead right-handed pull hitter is hitting. It will then be a second baseman's responsibility.

4. This can change, however, if it should be established that shortstop has a real weak arm. In that case, second baseman will make this play.

5. When going to bag to execute double play, charge the bag hard, and then hesitate slightly or shuffle to see in what direction throw is coming.

6. Tag the bag with left foot and shove off onto right as tag is being made.

7. When a poor throw to glove side, it may be necessary at times to throw left leg to the left and then tag with right foot, throwing as right foot touches bag.

8. When possible, come across bag to get out of way of runner.

9. Use the bag as a pushing off point.

10. Determine, based upon distance from bag, if a throw is necessary or if underhand toss will get the runner.

11. When using the underhand toss, give it to the shortstop firm. *A stiff wrist will increase accuracy.*

12. When ground ball is close enough to bag, tag bag himself; when not necessary, he should not handle ball twice. Stay in back of bag if he can on this play.

13. Not use the backhand toss when feeding ball to shortstop. Hard to control.

14. Not hide his throws. Only at one time will second baseman turn completely around; that is when a ball is hit real deep in hole to his left (very difficult).

15. No need to do a jump or full pivot when making double play. Catch ball, turn hips and upper part of body, bring hands and ball back, and throw.

16. *Draw a line in infield practice; one side of line must throw, other can toss.*

11

The First Baseman

The first baseman has three positions he must take. These positions will be taken depending upon:

1. Situation.
2. Inning.
3. Score.
4. Outs.
5. Hitter.

Deep Position:

1. Strong left-handed hitter.
2. Guard foul line when extra base hit will allow runner to score. Also, late in the game with a close score.

Halfway:

1. Over and to right with right-handed hitter hitting.
2. When bunt or push bunt type hitter hitting.

In:

1. When bunt definitely in order.

THE FIRST BASEMAN SHOULD:

1. Switch feet on thrown ball, if this is natural for individual.
   a.) Left-handed first baseman should throw to right, left foot on bag; throw to left, right foot on bag.
   b.) Right-handed first baseman should shift to left, right foot on bag; throw to right, left foot on bag; glove crosses over.
   c.) For a throw directly in center, either foot is acceptable.
2. Go to corner of bag in the direction throw is coming. No need to switch feet, however. Stretch and push off back leg.
3. *By always pushing off back leg (left-handed thrower, left leg; right-handed thrower,*

right leg), first baseman will always get maximum amount of reach.

4. Get in the habit of using one hand, except when poor throw in dirt.
5. Block all bad throws.
6. Remind pitcher when runner is taking too big a lead.
7. When tagging runner coming down line on a bad throw, do not jab at runner, but follow around with glove after tag has been made. Let runner tag himself out.
8. *When practicing drill to improve one-handed play, put throwing hand in back pocket and use only glove hand. Confidence will be built this way.*
9. *Knock all ground balls down, lie in front of them, and fall on knees if necessary. First base is close by, so play can always be made.*
10. Get in a habit of taking every throw as far out as he can. Don't catch ball in by chest; stretch out at all times. Don't let throw ride in.
11. Give pitcher good target for pick-off play.
12. Not be afraid to come off bag to make a play. This is a judgment play, and he will have to determine if he can get back in time.
13. Determine the range of second baseman.
14. Get all plays he can going to his right, however. (Pitcher will be covering.)
15. Yield to second baseman if play is easier for him.

Andre Thornton giving an excellent target. Base runner really has to stretch to get back in time. (top)

Craig Nettles cuts off another would-be hit. Notice the catlike reflexes he shows in pouncing on the ball and the perfect balance to unload to first. (right)

Jason Thompson has left leg planted on bag ready to push off for the throw. (left)

1

16. Call pitchers and catchers off all pop flies which are easier for him to make. Go to fence and screens; then come away to make catch.
17. When acting as cut-off man, stand sideways, hold hands up high,
18. *When acting as cut-off man and throw coming from center field, get up in front of mound so that throw won't hit mound or rubber and take a crazy hop.*
19. Always hustle to get himself in cut-off position early.
20. Not get too close to home plate as cut-off man. No value being too near.
21. When holding man on after pitcher has delivered ball, get into a fielding position.
22. As pitcher delivers, have body as much as possible in fair territory when holding man on; doesn't do any good on making a good play of a foul ball.
23. Listen for catcher's command when acting as cut-off man.
24. Keep throw out of line of runner when making throw to second base for double play. Keep outside. Take a step up or back depending upon time and speed of ball hit.
25. Make accurate throws.
26. When it is necessary for pitcher to cover first base, give pitcher ball as soon as possible.
27. *Give pitcher a firm underhand throw; stiff wrist will aid accuracy.*

2   3   4

28. Follow flight of ball to pitcher. Should he drop ball, then first baseman will be near to make play.
29. Advise pitchers of other runners on base, should they try to advance.
30. Follow runner to second base on sure double when second baseman and shortstop must act as cut-off men.
31. Guard foul line when extra base hit means an important run.
32. Run pitcher off topped balls, etc., when easier for first baseman to make play.
33. Shout to catcher, "There he goes," when runner stealing.
34. Make as many put-outs as possible when fielding ground ball when not necessary to make throw to pitcher. Don't take the chance of handling ball twice.
35. Know when bunt in order and charge ball.

There is a misconception in baseball that just about anyone can become a qualified first baseman. This is an untruth. To be a good first baseman it takes a lot of time and effort and good hard practice. Be the best.

12

The Third Baseman

The third baseman has three positions he must take: deep, halfway, in. The positions will be taken depending upon the score, outs, inning, situation, hitter.

1. Deep position should be taken when strong right-handed hitter is hitting.
2. Deep and guard foul line when extra base hit will allow runner to score.
3. Halfway and over when left-handed hitter is hitting.
4. Halfway in normal game situation when hitter has the ability to drag bunt.
5. Halfway when below average type hitter is hitting.
6. In when bunt is in order.
7. In when left-handed drag or push bunt type hitter hitting.
8. In and over when left-handed pull hitter hitting.

THE THIRD BASEMAN SHOULD:

1. Knock the ball down at all times.
2. Cut in front of shortstop and get all balls he can.
3. Throw ball over the top on all balls hit right at him and to his right.
4. When balls hit to his left, at times may be best for him to come from side.
5. Run pitchers and catchers off pop flies.
6. Go to fence and screen; then come away, allowing him to be in better position to catch pop flies.
7. Know what to do with ball before it is hit to him.
8. With men on first and second and ball hit to his left, go to second base for double play.
9. With men on first and second and ball hit to his right, tag third base, then go to first.

93

10. With bases loaded and double play in order, make play easiest way. To left, go to second base; to right, tag third base or go home. Ball right at him: second base, third base, or home, whichever is easiest.
11. Act as cut-off man when man on second and single to left field.
12. Act as cut-off man when runner on third base and fly ball to left field.
13. When acting as cut-off man, get self in position, left side of diamond between third base dirt area and home plate.
14. Hold hands high, giving outfielder a target to throw through.

15. Advise pitcher when runner getting too big a lead off third base.
16. Run pitcher off all topped balls that will be easier for third baseman to field.
17. Make play on topped ball with bare hand when necessary.
18. *When time allows, make small arc and come around, fielding topped ball so that you are facing first base, and third baseman will not have to throw across body.*
19. *Start creeping slowly as pitcher is about to release ball, getting body started; will aid in getting jump on ball.*
20. Not always cross over when ball is hit to his

1   2   3

left. Hard hit ball won't allow this.
21. Back up throws to pitcher after pick-off attempt when first baseman is returning ball to pitcher.
22. When going to right, plant foot and throw off it for strength and accuracy.
23. Throw from over top for strength and accuracy.
24. Encourage pitcher.
25. Be alert and ready for squeeze and alert pitcher for same.
26. Forget about talking to third base coach. He will only try and distract you.
27. *Topped and slow hit balls are toughest plays; practice them. Takes courage to play this position. Must be a take-charge guy. It's called the hot corner for good reason.*
28. Know how much ground the shortstop can cover.
29. Know the ability of the catcher to catch pop flies.
30. Know the fielding ability of each of your pitchers.

Aurelio Rodriguez comes up with a ball on the edge of the grass and guns down the runner. Notice how the pitcher gets down to make it easier for the third baseman to make a low, hard throw and also for the first baseman to pick the ball up quicker.

4

5

13

Outfielders

Like the infielder, every outfielder must say to himself, "Every ball hit is going to be hit to me. If I must go to my left, I am going here with the ball. If I must go to my right, I am going here with the ball." Prepare yourself mentally before every pitch; that way you will never be caught out to lunch.

BASIC OUTFIELD PROCEDURE:

1. During batting practice, shag balls in own position.
2. *Charge all ground balls, during the game as well as in batting practice.*
3. *Charge all ground balls directly at infielder. Even though it may look like a sure out, get in the habit of backing your infielders up.*
4. *Take only one step after catching ball; too many steps allow runners to advance. Poor throws are usually made after running with ball.*
5. When throwing, at all times follow through as would pitcher. Over-emphasize this when warming up and during infield practice. You will find this will strengthen your arm, as well as make it more accurate.
6. Charging ball will also allow you to get more on your throw.
7. Keep all throws low so that cut-off man can handle them.
8. Take one or two steps back from normal position. Then, as pitcher is about to release ball, start creeping just as infielder. This will help him get a great jump on the ball.
9. Keep off heels when running. Stay on balls of feet. Running on heels will cause eyes to bounce and cut down speed.
10. Know score, outs.
11. Don't throw behind runner. Know what base to throw to before ball is hit.
12. Don't allow tying or winning run to get into scoring position.
13. Know weaknesses and strengths of outfielders playing alongside of you.

97

14. *Shade yourself to the side you are weak going to.*
15. Back up all other outfielders.
16. Help other outfielders out verbally; constantly tell them what to do.
17. Run the infielders off of all the pop flies. The infielder will always come back until the outfielder runs him off.
18. In going to ball that will be near outfield fence, go to fence first and then come away. This will do away with many collisions.
19. All outfield fences are differently textured. Before game starts, check out how ball will come off fence, as well as how balls will react in corners. If open park, play deeper to cut off alleys.
20. Depending upon score, outs, how deep ball is hit, outfielder must decide when or when not to catch foul fly ball.

GETTING THE JUMP ON THE BALL AND CATCHING THE FLY BALL CORRECTLY

1. On ball hit to right side or over his head, the outfielder should, if right-handed thrower, pivot on right foot and then cross over. Ball hit to left side: step first with left leg, and then cross over with right. In both cases, make certain to shove hard off of back leg when making first step.
2. Left-handed throwers should do just the opposite: Take pivot on left foot; cross over with right leg when balls hit to their left. Step first with right leg when balls hit to their right; then cross over with left leg.
3. *Remember, everything you do in baseball, you do off your back leg.*
4. Don't trail the ball. Get yourself in position to field ball properly and make accurate, strong throws.
5. Always have one leg up in front slightly when taking outfield position.
6. On balls hit directly overhead, outfielder should pivot off back leg, then cross over as necessary.
7. Try to catch all fly balls with two hands.
8. Catch balls with back of glove toward face when ball above chest.
9. Catch balls with glove pocket facing sky when ball below chest.
10. Be relaxed. Let ball fall into glove; don't jar it.
11. All balls hit to the opposite field have a tendency to slice and head for foul lines. Be careful shagging the ball off of the opposite field hitter.
12. Depending upon the wind, sun, and other physical factors, determine what position you will take in outfield. Check these things out before game starts.
13. *Play as shallow as you possibly can. More base hits land in front of outfielder than do behind.*
14. When at all possible, outfielders should try and catch the ball on their throwing side.

In these two pictures, notice the outfielder catching the ball with both hands together by throwing shoulder for a quick release. Mickey Stanley backs him up, ready to holler where to throw the ball.

1   2

This will enable them to get rid of ball much quicker.

15. Hands can be resting on knees until pitch about ready to be made; then start creeping and bring hands off knees.

16. Run other outfielder off, should you be in a better position to throw.

OUTFIELD DRILLS

1. Throw overhand and follow through as pitcher would. Slap self in back with follow through hand.

2. Get as many ground balls as possible. If possible, shag grounders in infield, but do as a drill, not as a play period.

3. Pepper games are good for agility when played properly.

4. Practice the crossover even though you may not be shagging a ball.

5. Throw at extended distances for strengthening of arm throw.

6. *Line up with other outfielder about thirty feet away; toss ball over each other's head. This will help in determining proper way to go back on ball.*

7. Practice gripping ball across seams. Get in the habit of feeling ball correctly when making your throws.

8. Charge the ground balls; *charge ground balls.*

9. Run pitchers and all others out of your position during batting practice. This is the way you will learn to play. *Play it alone.*

10. Practice catching ball off throwing foot. This saves a step, and if ball is high enough, this can be done.

11. Practice on short step when catching both ground ball and fly ball. You can't throw anyone out if you can run with ball.

12. Get yourself a good big glove. Put it on your hand; don't let it lay loosely.

13. Run, run, run—an outfielder is only as good as his legs.

part 2
The Offense in Baseball

14

Charlie Lau on Hitting

Charlie Lau, hitting coach, New York Yankees.

Considering the importance of batting in baseball, it's astonishing how few major league teams employ full-time batting coaches. That's why, perhaps, every time a batting coach achieves some success, he's immediately hailed as a "genius." To name a few: Paul Waner, George Sisler, Harry Walker, Wally Moses, Ted Williams.

Major league baseball's current batting guru is Charlie Lau of the New York Yankees. Under his tutelage, the Yankees have become famous as a smart, sharp-hitting team. And, supreme accolade, a lot of hitters from other clubs are now coming to them for advice.

Lau has the master teacher's way about him—a slow and easy way of talking and making his points. He takes one point at a time and ingrains it through repetition.

Like most great teachers, he's more than a technician. He's also a master psychologist. He

103

"Hand position" is the key point as the front foot completes the stride. Craig Nettles shows how the hands and bat are back at the letters at this key position.

has the ability to make his players respect and believe in him.

For example, while talking hitting one evening, he introduced us to a nearby Royal player in this fashion: "This man isn't playing much right now, but he certainly can hit and he can go to the opposite field in splendid fashion."

The player beamed. His day had been made and you could bet that he was going to be more open than ever to any suggestion from his hitting coach.

Another Royal player sat on the steps of the dugout and asked if it would be all right to listen in on our seminar on hitting; it would serve as a refresher course for him. The player, John Wathan, showed a real major-league attitude—and the kind of respect he had for his hitting coach.

Charlie, what is your basic method of teaching hitting?

I am a strong believer in the mechanics. Anyone who can execute them properly should be able to hit the baseball with authority—assuming, of course, he has decent eyesight, reflexes, strength, and the dedication to work and work on his hitting. I might also add courage. Everyone has to overcome, or control, the fear of being hit with the ball.

What do you consider to be the vital mechanics of hitting?

First and foremost is watching the ball all the way to the bat—keeping the head still and concentrating totally on the ball.

Next, you must be balanced before the swing, during the swing, and after contact.

"Balance" is a key word. Your weight must be over your toes, the waist slightly bent forward, hands comfortable (without tension), knees slightly flexed (to promote relaxation), and the bat leveled off at the back, almost parallel with the ground.

A balanced weight shift at the proper time will eliminate tightness and tension and bring the weight into the swing, allowing you to hit with authority.

Whether it's baseball, boxing, football, or almost any other sport, good balance makes you quicker. Watch any of the outstanding athletes and you'll see how balanced they are most of the time.

What other points in the stance do you emphasize, and do you prefer one stance over another?

We like to work from a closed or parallel stance and, as I've said, with a bend in the waist for balance and relaxation. If you're not relaxed, you can't be fluid. Standing up straight causes tension.

One of the things you must watch for is a very wide stance that makes it difficult for the hitter to keep his weight back. If the hitter is having trouble this way, you may have him bring his feet close together. This will help him keep his weight back. Al Cowens is a great example of this.

You mentioned that you want the bat to be leveled off behind the head, almost parallel with the ground. Would you elaborate on this?

A lot of hitters cock the bat too high or hold it way back away from their body. It's pointless. You can't start the swing from that position. You must move the bat down to level out the swing, and this takes time. So why not start from this position to begin with?

A level bat position will reduce the tension and tightness in your arms and hands and enable you to wait longer for the pitch, as your bat is all ready to be brought forward. You'll proba-

bly meet the ball squarely and probably hit line drives.

How do you go about teaching the stride?

Again, the main thing is to be in balance after the stride. As your front foot touches the ground, your hands must be way back near the letters, not starting forward.

A while back, we put separate cameras on the pitchers and hitters and we found that just as the pitcher comes to his release point, the hitter must react with his hands to get the bat in position to hit. (Note: At this point, Tom Poquette, who had been listening in the dugout, said that he thought this fact was amazing.)

I shot all the hitters in the 1973 All-Star game at sixty frames per second, and I found that every one of them, no matter how unorthodox his style or where he started his swing, had one thing in common in their strides: as the front (striding) foot completed its stride, the hands and bat were back at the letters.

I call this the "hands position." It means the hands must be back in the launching position as the front foot hits the ground.

What other mechanics do you stress?

We are great believers in full-arm extension. We like to emphasize swinging on top of the ball (chopping down on the ball). I used to think Cesar Cedeno really chopped down on the ball, but super slow-motion pictures of his hitting style show that he comes almost level on the ball. This amazed me after seeing him hit.

How do you teach going to the opposite field?

If you're relaxed without much tension in your arms and hands, it's easy to let the hands lead the bat through the plate area and swing inside out.

How would you correct for a hand hitch?

A hitch down may be all right, but a hitch up with your hands is a real detriment. You may help the hitter overcome this by having him level out the bat behind him and rest it on his shoulder.

What about the top hand or dominant hand in hitting?

Some hitters have a really dominant or much

1 2 3 4 5

stronger hand. Usually it's the top hand (right hand for right-handers, left hand for left-handers). This hand will take over after contact and prevent a full-arm extension or cause too much hand, wrist, and arm roll.

We sometimes advocate releasing that hand after contact. That's why Willie Horton appears to hit so many home runs with one arm. He releases the other hand after driving through and making contact with the ball.

How do you increase bat speed, and how much emphasis do you put on keeping that front shoulder closed?

If all of the mechanics are right and you attain the ultimate—a perfect swing—then the above things will take care of themselves.

Perfection in hitting is attained with relaxation, elimination of tension and tightness, total concentration, balance at all times, good position far enough away from the plate so you step in to the pitch, a shifting of weight at the proper time, bat leveled off, eyes on the ball, head still, stride or front foot down, the hands back in the launching position, arms fully extended, and the hitter mentally prepared—knowing what the pitcher can do and where he (hitter) is going to hit the ball.

John Mayberry. Though the big first baseman does not subscribe fully to the "Lau method"—he stands more erect and cocks his bat a bit higher—he still produces a beautiful and powerful arc with his bat. Note how he keeps everything back at about shoulder level as he strides, and how he keeps his front shoulder turned in. His powerful hip and shoulder drive brings his weight behind the bat, as he drives off the outside of his front foot and comes up on the back toe. Look at the "L" formed by his back and rear leg and how his head never moves; his eyes stay trained on the pitch all the way.

6   7   8

What about the mental aspects of hitting?

Tonight, Dennis Eckersley (a right-hander) is going for the Indians. He's a power pitcher who deals in smoke with two different types of fast balls. So George Brett (a left-handed hitter) is going to shut the hitting area from second base to the right-field line out of his mind. He's going to concentrate on hitting every pitch into the area from second base to left-field line. Anything else he gets will be a bonus.

Too many hitters try to pull the pitch, even if it's on the outside part of the plate. You must think: cover the outside of the plate first, go to the middle second, and cover the inside part of the plate last. Hit the ball where it is pitched.

Still thinking about the mental aspects, should your thinking be dictated by the dimensions of the park in which you're playing?

Some home parks have outfields as large as airports, and you're not going to put many into the cheap seats. So your swing should be dictated by this factor. Major league pitchers make a living by generally pitching the hitters away.

What are the most common faults of Little League and high school hitters?

The most common fault is taking the eyes off the ball much too soon. This is usually accompanied by a premature turning of the head—jerking the head out of the swing.

(Note: Later in the evening Lau called us out to the batting cage and pointed out the principle that his hitters were working on—trying to see the ball hit the bat. "Total concentration," Lau said, "is all we're working on in batting practice." . . . "He saw that one pretty good." . . . "No, he did not watch that one very well." . . . "If a hitter sees that ball all the way in batting practice, chances are he'll do the same in the game.")

The second biggest mistake of a lot of young hitters is standing too close to the plate. If the pitch comes in close, they then have to step away from it, jerking their head out too soon—compounding the problems of trying to keep the head still and the eyes on the ball all the way to the bat. Pulling away may cause them to lose sight of the ball.

The other problem, of course, is that any pitch in tight to the hitter may increase his fear of getting hit, and he'll tend to open up too soon or bail out.

I'd much rather have the young hitter stand farther from the plate and move into every pitch. This will facilitate his shift and give him a better chance to follow the pitch.

What hitting drills do you use?

The batting tee is excellent for developing your stroke and seeing where the ball should be hit. Tossing the ball underhanded and hitting it is another good drill. It certainly improves your stroke groove.

The best hitting drill is having the hitter go into the batting cage and stand and swing through a couple of times, like a pendulum. As the pitcher starts to wind, the batter brings the bat back to the launching position freely, and then goes immediately into the swing. This removes all tension and the hitter can do what he is supposed to do with the bat.

While working with the hitter in the batting cage, you can help him determine just when to start shifting his weight and whether he's a front-foot or back-foot hitter. He must be balanced in either case and he must shift his weight

1

at the right time, without any tension and tightness in his body and arms.

How do you approach the individual hitter?

I check his build, size, coordination, reaction time, strength, speed, and then try to get him to use what he's got—to get the most out of his native ability and size.

A small man will have a better chance of getting a perfect swing more consistently than a big man, but when the big man does get a perfect swing, he'll hit the ball a lot farther than the small man. But it's much harder for that big man to get that perfect swing together.

Though not a New York Yankee, the great Rod Carew follows all of Charlie Lau's principles. All that "puttering around" in the first three photos is quite meaningful. It is in line with Lau's theory of mental preparation. "You've got to be thinking of how to settle your weight, whether you're a front-foot or back-foot hitter, how high your bat is cocked, etc. A golfer will go up to the tee and take two minutes to set up. A hitter will go up and just dig in, thinking he's ready. He rarely will be. He hasn't thought everything out." Note how relaxed and balanced Carew is, and how he keeps the bat almost leveled off where he can completely control it.

2

3

4

5

6

7

15
Ralph Kiner on Hitting

Every baseball person knows Ralph Kiner. One of the three or four greatest home-run hitters in history, he is now an outstanding broadcaster who makes the game come alive with his insight and lucidness.

As a youngster, I remember Kiner's short, compact stroke and towering home runs. His times at bat per home run is the third best of all time: 14.11 to Babe Ruth's 11.76 and Harmon Killebrew's 13.74. He is the only man ever to lead the league in home runs seven consecutive years.

The image of the home-run hitter is a super-strong athlete who can hunt bears with a switch. Ralph Kiner brought an extra dimension to his craft—he studied hitting deeply and improved on his natural talents. He was the first player to use a golf glove to secure a better grip and eliminate slipping.

Long before television and video tape, Ralph had someone film his swing with an 8-mm. camera at 64 frames per second. He then studied his form frame by frame to check on his mechanics. He also kept a card catalog on every pitcher he faced. Obviously, he was one of the first ardent students of hitting. Kiner has remained contemporary on hitting by serving as hitting instructor with the New York Mets.

The following are Kiner's seven checkpoints to successful hitting. Properly applied, they should help anyone hit well. The neglect of even one can cause trouble.

1. Proper use of master, or focusing, eye
2. Weight transference to the front leg
3. Up on the back toe
4. Arms fully extended when hitting
5. Front shoulder kept in
6. Two halves (upper body and lower body) coordinating properly
7. Observation of the "L" principle

A young Ralph Kiner demonstrating proper knuckle alignment, position at the batter's box, and splendid contact with full arm extension.

Mike Schmidt of the Phillies demonstrates a short, compact hitting stroke with perfect arm extension and follow-through. Schmidt in the third photo has lowered his hands for the low pitch. (You can see the ball in the right part of the picture.) He has slightly lowered his body to zero in on the ball.

Let us explore his principles in depth. First, the master, or focusing, eye principle. It is simple to determine your master eye. Hold your hand fully extended in front of your face, with your index finger and thumb in a circle. Look at the circle with both eyes open. Then close one eye. If the circle does not move, the open eye is your master eye.

For most right-handed hitters, the right eye is the master eye and this eye must be on the ball. The hitter must, however, make sure that he can see the pitcher with both eyes, and that the eyes are on a level plane.

Check the accompanying pictures of Stan Musial. Note his open mouth. Many people thought he smiled when he hit (which he had a right to do!). Actually, he kept his mouth open so that he could see the pitcher better. Try it. Open your mouth and try to blink your eyes at the same time. It isn't that simple. You thus minimize losing sight of the ball for even a split second. Incidentally, the open mouth also relaxes the lower face. I asked Kiner the following questions:

Is it possible to watch the ball right up to the point it meets the bat?

No, I don't think there ever was a player who could see the bat hit the ball. By tremendous concentration, you can follow it up to about a foot from the bat or a little closer if it is met on the outside part of the plate. But the speed of the bat and the ball prohibits seeing the actual contact.

What is your theory in regard to shifting the weight from the back foot to the front foot?

Baseball is no different from any other sport. In shooting a basketball, you shift the weight from back to front. In hitting a tennis ball, you shift the weight from back foot to front foot. The same principle applies in golf, football passing, shot-putting, etc.

One of the most misunderstood things in hitting is that you stay on your back foot but shift your weight to the front foot. This is the most important thing in hitting.

Why is it so important to get your weight off the back foot?

If you hit with your back heel on the ground,

you'll never be able to turn your hips. It is interesting that Tony Oliva injured his back foot a couple of seasons ago and had to get up on his back toe. He then started hitting with a great deal of power.

An excellent way to teach this: put an old baseball under the hitter's back heel and have him take his normal swing. This will make him get up on his back toe and pivot.

Anytime the hitter can shift his weight off the back foot and get his back heel off the ground, his hips will turn. Hitting with the back heel on the ground makes him drop everything underneath the ball and uppercut it.

The hitter who is late transferring his weight forward and getting his heel off the ground is going to get behind the pitch. His hands and his hips won't be able to function properly.

The front arm (left for right-handed hitter) represents another key point in hitting. It must be straight. Anytime a hitter gets caught with his arms bent, it means that he has not put the bat far enough up to the ball.

So the hitter has to work at getting a full extension of the left arm. Look at the picture of Boog Powell, which shows a perfect arm extension. This allows him to make contact with the ball out in front of his body.

The ball must be hit from two to eighteen inches out in front of the hitter. Why such a variance? Because inside pitches must be met farther out in front. Outside pitches can be hit farther back.

Paul Waner's remedy for a hitch was having the hitter reach back as far as he could with his front arm and then swinging from there.

Dick Howser of the Yankees has a great way of teaching this full-arm extension and increasing bat speed. Take your full hard swing with a leaded bat (40 to 70 ounces), allowing the bat to follow through. Hold for a split second, then snap the bat back as fast and hard as you can to the starting position. It is like running a movie projector backward. Repeat this 50 to 150 times, without resting or dropping your arms. Although very tiring, it really does the job. It is a great drill for developing bat speed and learning to pop that bat with a full arm extension.

The next key point in hitting is the front shoulder. This should stay in position. Some of the experts thought that Roberto Clemente had

Stan Musial's unique style stressed cocked stance, relaxed position, knees and body. In photo 2, check the square shoulders and hips, head right in there, step into the plate, relaxed knees, extended front arm, and everything held back for the actual swing. Three excellent points in the next photo to note just after contact: the still head, the arm extension, and the "L" formed at the knee of the back leg. The last picture shows beautifully free arm action and the "L" formed at the knee of the back leg. *Photos by Alfred Fleishman.*

Perfect bat position a moment after contact. Look at all that power Dick Allen is putting behind his swing, as well as the classic "L" in the back leg and the still head. The ball will be met out in front.

Boog Powell illustrates super arm extension after the swing. Also check his head and eyes—they are still trained on the ball.

1

2

3

5

6

Greg Luzinski's driving swing is a real power stroke. Notice in picture 2 how his front arm is fully extended back, with little or no bend. This was Lloyd Waner's way to eliminate a hand hitch. (See Chapter 14.) Photo 5 shows everything going into the ball.

1

2

3

4

5

6

Thurman Munson says, "I hit to score runs." Munson is very quick with his hands. Notice in the second photo the perfect position of his hands and how quick he brings them into the pitch. Notice in the last few photos his quick start for first.

1

2

3

4

5

George Foster attacking the low pitch and hitting it with authority. Study this sequence and see how many excellent fundamentals you can find.

6

1

2

Reggie Jackson shows the classic swing in photos 3 and 4, as he swings down on a high pitch. Reggie likes to whip his bat like a fly swatter, handling it in a highly effective manner. He wants to sting the ball out in front of himself.

3

4

5

6

7

8

a very unorthodox swing. True, he pulled away with his front foot, but basically he had one of the best swings I have ever seen. Clemente would "step in the bucket," but he'd keep the upper part of his body closed.

Many poor hitters turn the front shoulder out. The only pitch this kind of hitter can handle is a fast ball. The curve or off-speed pitch will force him completely out of position.

This brings us to another checkpoint—the body being cut in half at the waist, making two pieces to the swing.

The upper part of the body hardly moves, although it may turn somewhat with the stride. The lower part of the body does the work. You hold the front shoulder as steady as possible and work from the bottom around.

The steady front shoulder also keeps the head in and still, which is essential. So, no matter what the pitch, you will be able to handle it.

The right arm is a very important part of the swing, and the right elbow is the checkpoint. It should be in a hitting position away from the body.

The "L" is the final checkpoint—all the good hitters observe this mechanic, as you have already seen in the illustrations. The L is formed by the back toe, leg, hip, and back as contact with the ball is made.

Mentally, the key to being a good hitter is to get your pitch and hit it. With no strikes, the hitter who swings at a low outside curve or a high inside fast ball is playing right into the pitcher's hands.

16

Bunting

One of the most important and probably the most poorly executed plays in baseball is the bunt. More games have been lost because of someone failing to advance a man than perhaps any other reason. Let's attempt to understand proper bunting fundamentals.

As with everything else in baseball, the starting point is the back foot. It is necessary for the bunter to turn on the ball of his back foot. I do not mean the back foot brought up even with the front. It is a spin; actually, all that turns completely is the upper part of the body. This move does away with completely jumping around. By moving only the upper part of the body, you can actually stay in your hitting position and get yourself ready that much quicker from there.

As you turn the upper part of your body, your knees should automatically bend slightly and your bat should come into position covering home plate. The arms should not be extended, but should be slightly bent and relaxed. Bat on a forty-five-degree angle and out in front of home plate. Hold the bat loosely, and don't jab at the ball; let the ball come to you. As in hitting, make sure you get a good ball to bunt.

The top hand should be the contact hand, bat held just about on the trademark. Use the top hand just as if you were going to catch the ball with it. In other words, top hand goes to the ball; bottom hand works as a lever and by pushing or pulling will determine what side ball will be bunted on.

Remember:
1. Get a good ball to bunt.
2. Have bat out in front of plate and cover plate.
3. Don't stick your tail out; stay up at the plate.

Bunting for a base hit, Willie Randolph style.

Notice in these pictures that Rivers doesn't show his intention of drag bunting until the last possible second. Also notice in photo 2 where his top hand is. Photo 3 shows the key to drag bunting; he is using the crossover and stepping toward the pitcher.

4. Bend knees slightly.
5. Aim for foul lines.
6. Make the *right* man field the ball.
7. Top hand makes the contact, bottom hand does the guiding.

Both drag and push bunting are an important part of the game and should be practiced, especially by the light-hitting player who may have the speed where a good bunt or two a ball game can help him become a much better player. The drag and push bunter also should use the top hand as the catching hand (laying bat on ball). Practice and say to yourself, "I will catch this ball with my top hand." You will soon see how your bunts will improve. Again, aim for foul lines.

The right-handed hitter pushes the ball by the pitcher to make the second baseman field the ball. This is done from the hitting stance. Slide the right hand up on the bat; hold the bat rather firm. Most success is obtained with an outside pitch.

The real key to being a successful drag bunter is that the hitter must *take his first step directly toward the pitcher with a crossover step,* not away from the plate, so that he can bunt the ball if it is an outside pitch or change of pace pitch.

To perfect all types of bunting each player must practice them as much as possible.

Bunting. Notice how the bunter has lowered his body, keeping his bat parallel with the ground.

3

4

17

Base Running

There are three important phases of base running: stealing bases, running on a batted ball from batter's box, and after player becomes a base runner.

STEALING BASES

This phase of base running can be used to the best advantage by the men on the team adept at stealing bases.

1. The lead off base is important—make sure there is equal distribution of weight on both feet so that you can go either way (back to the base or advance) without loss of time. The first quick step is a crossover, regardless of the way you go.
2. Base leads are governed by the number of outs and the game situation.
   a.) Always stay inside the fielder with bases loaded and no outs. Never get caught on line drive. If on third, line drives below pitcher's waist will hit the ground; above can be caught.
   b.) Each base runner should get as much lead as he can; a lead has to be fought for.
   c.) Know the pitcher's moves.
   d.) Lead on second in bunt situation should guard against getting picked off if ball is missed—two steps and back with the pitch.
   e.) Strive for a walking lead.
   f.) Base stealers should try for maximum lead on every pitch to keep from tipping off the pitch they will be stealing on.
   g.) A half-step can be gained by crossing over on the initial step.
3. Study the move of every pitcher (this can be done when you are on the bench as well as

Getting a lead off second. In photo 1, runner is on bag while catcher is giving signs. In photos 2–5, he edges off toward third. Notice in photos 6 and 7 how his front foot is just barely touching down, ready to go if the ball is hit on the ground to the right side of the infield. Also note in 7 and 8 that he is in perfect position to cross over and get back to second base.

1

5

when you are a base runner). The pitcher may lean toward the plate, rock, raise his front foot too high, or look at the runner only once before delivering the ball—any of these characteristics may be the base runner's key to advance. Study the mannerisms of the infielders; you can steal on them at times.

4. Double steal

    a.) Men on first and third. The runner on first breaks for second as in straight steal; runner on third holds his lead off third until he sees the ball in flight, then breaks for home. With no one out or one out, the runner on first always goes through; with two out, he holds up to give man on third a chance to score.

    b.) Men on first and second. The runner on first has to wait to break until the runner on second breaks for third.

    c.) Delayed double steal. Man on first breaks just as the catcher is about to release the ball in throwing back to the pitcher. This can best be attempted when shortstop and second baseman are playing wide of second base and deep.

RUNNING ON A BATTED BALL FROM THE BATTER'S BOX

If player is not adept at stealing bases, it can be helpful in developing good base running skills by following a routine. Remember: all players should possess some knowledge of base running.

1. *Run hard* to first base every time the ball is hit. When ball is hit to the outfield, make the turn at first base as if every base hit has a two-base possibility.

2. Safeguard against making the wide sweeping turns around the bases. Touch the bag with the *left* foot whenever possible, but if the player cannot hit the bag with the left foot on the inside of the bag, he should not break stride to do so. Get in the base line (straight line between each base or as close to a straight line as possible) after passing each base.

3. Which of the opposing outfielders can throw well?

4. Where do my opponents play for batter?

5. Is the outfielder handling the batted ball a right- or left-hander? (If the ball is handled on the off side, usually the glove hand, the outfielder will take a little more time to throw the ball. This makes it possible for runner to gain a step or more on the batted ball.)

Player should always run with his head up. He can follow the play better. If the ball is hit out of his vision or behind him (to right field or possible triple), look at the third base coach when approximately thirty feet from second base for the signal to stop or continue to third base. Runner should rely on his own judgment when play is in front of him.

AFTER PLAYER BECOMES A BASE RUNNER

1. *Never* get caught on line drive with *no* outs.
2. Always keep in mind the number of outs.
3. Find out who has the ball. (If the pitcher is on the mound and near the rubber he must have possession of the ball; otherwise it is a balk.)
4. Look for a possible sign (hit and run or steal).
5. Know where you're going when a ball is hit.
6. Get a reasonable, comfortable lead. (Don't lean toward second base or appear anxious to go if hit and run play is on—this may tip off the play to an observing opponent.)
7. Follow the ball from the pitcher's hand to the batter and either advance as the ball comes in contact with the bat or, if the ball

is not hit, *go back to base as quickly as possible* to safeguard against being caught in the base line on a possible pick-off play.

8. If advancing on a hit and run play, the player should glance over his left shoulder to see where the ball is hit—if he cannot *find* the ball he should look at his coaches for a signal where to go and what to do. The player should not allow the opposing infielder to decoy him into believing the ball is hit on the ground, if it is hit in the air.

9. To break up the double play (at second base): Some infielders find it difficult to get out of the base line when handling the ball at second base on the possible double play, second to first. The runner is entitled to the base line—always slide into second base on this play; this makes it difficult for the man handling the ball to get it away to first base in time to complete the play.

10. Runners tag up on all foul flies whether infield or outfield. This is a rule that must be followed.

11. Never get caught going from second to third on ball hit to left side.

12. A good base runner has to be daring, but not foolish, and know his own speed and limitations.

13. Never get tagged by second baseman with one out and a man on first and third.

14. Take walking lead off third base. It isn't important how far you get off the bag; just be sure to be moving toward home plate when ball is hit. When returning to bag, *always* come back to third on the inside of the bag or line. On offense, we like to go home on any ground ball.

15. *Never* take your club out of an inning trying to go from first to third with two outs.

HAVE YOUR COACHES AND BASE RUNNERS REMIND THEMSELVES!

1. Where is the ball?
2. How many are there out? Know the game situation.
3. Look for a possible sign.
4. Don't talk to the opposing infielders (or to the umpires). Often this is done to distract your attention and may cost the player a base he might otherwise have advanced.
5. Players should always run with their heads up.
6. Always tag up on all foul flies.
7. *Touch all bases.*
8. Run using arms as pistons in front of body.
9. Always run on toes, not flat-footed.
10. Watch runner in front of you.
11. When in doubt, always slide, especially if there is a play.
12. Most base runners get lazy and then wonder why they are thrown out by one step.

18

Sliding Fundamentals

Sliding is a fundamental which should be taught not only for its offensive use but to prevent injuries. Many times a player will have advanced quite far in baseball, but because he has not perfected his sliding, he will injure himself and be out for a good part of the season. This is the reason some players on the major league level use only head first slides; they simply can't slide the other way.

Sliding at a young age (nine or ten) can be learned expertly in a relatively short time. One of the best ways is through the use of a sliding pit. (Make one by excavating a 16-foot square in one corner of the field to a depth of 3 or 4 feet. Fill with fine sand, and anchor a strap in the exact center of this pit so that the strap comes up through the sand, and to which a base may be attached. Create runways from two directions so that the player may come down the runways and slide, without injury, to the base.

Another effective way to teach sliding is to take your team out in the outfield grass after a rain. Have them wear old pants or a pair of shorts over sweatpants, and have them take their shoes off and work on sliding. They have a lot of fun sliding on the wet grass and really get the feel of what sliding is like. Some major leaguers wear hitting gloves on both hands to keep their hands from getting scraped up.

You may want to have your players make fists by grabbing a handful of grass in each hand or a small amount of dirt. This will prevent injury from jamming of hands into the ground when sliding. It helps to prevent injury to the wrist and fingers.

The bent leg is the safest in baseball and can be used as a hook (both right and left), the straight-in, and the pop-up slide. The player slides on the calf of the bent leg, which must be on the bottom.

1. Take off from either leg (whichever is most natural) and bend it under.

133

2. Always tag the base with "top" leg. Keep the knee slightly bent and the heel well off the ground.

3. When teaching the hook slide, have your players use the top leg when going to the right or left side.

4. When going straight in, shove top leg straight at the bag.

Have your players stay close to the ground and not leap or jump. A slide is a glide. Teach your players to throw their heads back as they bend both legs. This keeps knees from hitting ground first.

Other key teaching points for your players:

1. Have them start their slide six to eight feet from the bag. Do not slide late and have them jam themselves against the bag.

2. Ride the calf or bottom leg at all times.

3. All slides can be done well only with speed.

4. To accomplish pop-up slide, have players lift themselves up as they slide along with speed.

5. Teach players the straight-in, hook, and pop-up slides thoroughly; then work on the clever slides later.

6. Try and pick up the coach when sliding into third base.

7. When catcher is straddling home plate, go in straight and between his legs.

8. If your player finds himself sliding late, try having him raise his body into a pop-up slide as he hits the bag. This will take the jar out when sliding into a bag which is anchored in the ground.

9. Whenever in doubt, always have your players slide.

10. Many careers are ended by poor sliding. Spend enough practice time so your players can perfect their sliding.

1

This sequence shows excellent take-off, gliding on the calf of the leg with a good pop-up at the end. Safe or out?

2

3

19

Getting It All Together in Practice

Baseball practice must be fun, interesting, and challenging in order to develop a high degree of excellence. It must also simulate game conditions as much as possible, be fast-paced, varied, and give each player an opportunity to sharpen his skills to the best of his ability. Constant repetition of the correct techniques will enable the player to do the right thing instinctively.

Practices can be adapted to whatever aspect of the game the coach wishes to emphasize—offensive, defensive, a combination, or simply fun time (after an especially tough loss or letdown following examinations or a heavy emotional experience).

Although it is impossible to include all drills every day, we pick the ones that the team needs most at that particular stage of the season. A typical early-season practice has the players warm up with some running and each man doing some stretching exercises to loosen all of his muscles. Our thinking here was influenced

by Percy Cerutty and the European soccer players who warm up almost entirely by stretching.

We then do some catching and pepper to warm up the throwing arms. A typical early-season practice would go as follows:

2:00-2:15: Individual drills.
2:15-2:20: Burma Road (explained later), a conditioning or base-running drill.
2:20-2:35: Team defensive drill—double cut-off (against first-and-third attempted double steal) and defensing the squeeze play.
2:35-3:40: Hitting drills—eight swings and two bunts: (1) 0-2 count (choke up on the bat, shorten stroke, and widen strike zone); (2) move runner over to third from second with nobody out; and (3) squeeze play.
3:40-3:50: Timed base running, touching all bases (13.2 to 14.5 seconds is excellent).
3:50-4:05: Infield or situation drills.
4:05-4:10: Burma Road.

(Above) Individual practice time, twenty minutes. A tremendous drill for improving defensive play of your team. Pitchers in foreground are doing pick-ups. Shortstop and second baseman are working on the double play. First basemen are working on the throws in the dirt. Catchers are shifting to throw to second. Outfielders are charging ground balls and coming up throwing. Third baseman is catching popups in foul territory. Vary drill with each group every day, and you'll be able to cover all aspects of defensive play.

Same drill on different day (below). Third basemen are charging slow hit balls along the line. Pitchers are working with first baseman on slow hit balls to first baseman's right. Outfielders are hitting to shortstop and second baseman on cut-off throws. Catchers are firing out on bunts in front of the plate.

Let us take a closer look at each component of the practice. We generally like to start practice with individual position drills, but this varies from time to time. We want to create as many game situations as possible and work on them every day. We also do a lot of small-group work at the same time. In fact, we bring the squad together only when everyone is needed. This gives each player many more chances to improve a certain technique. For example, in eight minutes an individual can get twenty double-play opportunities. The following are some individual drills we work on.

THIRD BASEMEN

1. A string of fifteen balls is laid down between third and home (parallel with the foul line), and each third baseman charges in and scoops up the balls—one at a time—and throws to first.

 Once the players become adept, we have someone roll the balls very slowly at them to give them practice at scooping up the topped ball or bunt.
2. Pop flies near third and home.
3. Protecting the foul line in late innings.
4. Fielding hard-hit ground balls to the left.
5. Backhanding balls hit to the right.
6. Holding runner on third.
7. Following runner in on squeeze play.
8. Charging bunt with runners on first and second (force play at third with shortstop covering third).
9. Cutting in front of shortstop to take any ball he can reach.
10. Putting the tag on runners.
11. Playing deep with a force situation at third.
12. Double plays from third to second to first.
13. Hot-box situations with catcher. (Also with shortstop and second baseman.)
14. Taking throws from outfielders and putting the tag on.
15. Cut-off situations.

SECOND BASEMEN AND SHORTSTOPS

1. Double plays on balls hit in the hole at short, right at the shortstop, and to his left on medium and soft ground balls.
2. Roll a wooden barrel over second base to simulate a runner trying to break up a double play. You will be surprised at how much quicker your keystone pair will learn to get rid of the ball. They will develop a feel for getting out of the way of the runner.
3. Double plays from second to short to first on balls hit to second baseman's right, left, and directly at him.
4. Stretching on force plays at second.
5. Pop flies back of second baseman and shortstop (work with outfielders).
6. Pick-off plays at second working with pitchers.
7. Keeping runners close to second.
8. Double cut-off situations (both men out on extra-base hits in the alleys).
9. Cut-off positioning and relay throws.
10. Charging topped balls from a deep position.
11. Hot-box situations.
12. Comeback double plays—pitcher to shortstop (or second basemen) to first.

FIRST BASEMEN

1. Stretching drills on throws (opposite leg from glove hand to assure maximum stretch).
2. Shifting on bad throws, left and right.

Individual drill shows catchers working on blocking balls in the dirt.

1

2

3

4

5

This drill for a pivoting infielder is one of the finest for developing quick hands and getting rid of the ball. A feeder will have about twenty balls in front of him on the ground and start feeding them one at a time to the pivot man, who will throw into a screen or backstop. As he gets better, you increase the speed with which you feed him. When he really becomes adroit around the bag, have him fold his glove fingers in and catch the ball with the back of his glove. His bare hand is always working to develop surer and quicker hands with a fast release. Another ball will be on the way to him as he releases the ball in the last photo.

In this sequence, the young ballplayer has a lead baseball (same size as a regular baseball but weighing between five and eight pounds) in his pitching hand. In photo 2, he stands on his tiptoes and extends his arm as far as possible. In the final picture, he is gripping the lead ball with his fingertips and then turning it in his hand and on his fingertips, just as if he were screwing a light bulb in a socket. Begin with 5 repetitions and gradually build up to 150. This is one of the best drills to build up your arm and the ligaments and tendons in your pitching elbow.

These two pitching sequences illustrate an excellent way to teach a young pitcher how to get his body into the pitch. One youngster holds the other's back ankle loose enough so he can pivot and go to the plate. Notice how the body comes completely through and behind the pitch in the last two photos. It is not necessary to have a baseball in this drill, but by doing this dry run 50 to 100 times every day, from the stretch and wind-up, you will soon have the feel of what it is like to pitch and use your whole body, not just your arm. Your pitching form will become second nature and much easier on your arm. The second photo sequence shows the same drill from the left side.

This sequence shows an excellent individual drill practice session. In the background, first basemen are working on digging the ball out of the dirt. In the middle, pitchers are stretching and charging bunts on the first base line. Catchers are working on throws to second, and third basemen will work on slow-hit topped baseballs off the plate.

The start of the Burma Road, everybody's favorite conditioning drill. On this leg, the young men sprint to first, as the second group waits its turn. Notice the all-out effort and keen competition among the teammates. A splendid conditioner and a great way to finish up practice on an upbeat. Burma Road also improves base running.

Another drill with the lead baseball which will help the flexibility and strength of your throwing hand. Notice that he is supporting his throwing arm with his other hand as he slowly moves his wrist, fingers, and hand forward and then backward through the full range of movement. Start with 10 and gradually increase until you can do 200 each day.

3. Throwing the ball in the dirt to each other—short hops, long hops, and in between hops.
4. Jumping for high throws and making a slap tag (bending both knees before throw arrives).
5. Throws inside and down the line.
6. Pop flies from behind first to the plate.
7. Working on balls hit to his right and feeding the pitcher (overhand and underhand).
8. Double plays on ball hit behind and in front of first, with shortstop covering second.
9. Charging and fielding bunts.
10. Protecting the foul line on balls hit to his left (late innings).
11. Cut-off situations.
12. Work with catcher on dropped third strikes.

CATCHERS

1. Blocking balls thrown in the dirt.
2. Shifting for throw to second, stepping with right foot first.
3. Shifting and throwing to third with right-handed hitter at bat.
4. Blocking the plate and making tags.
5. Taking throws from outfielder at plate—short, medium, and long hops.
6. Feeding pitcher covering the plate on wild pitches or passed balls with runner on third.
7. Pop fouls back of and in front of plate.
8. Fielding bunts in front of plate.
9. Dropped third strike.
10. Pick-off at first base.

OUTFIELDERS

1. Charging ground balls and throwing to a relay man.
2. Blocking ground balls.
3. Going for balls hit over head (crossover step and go).
4. Handling ball lost in the sun (step to one side or the other). Work with sunglasses also.
5. Call drills with all three outfielders.
6. Call drills between center fielder and right fielder.
7. Call drill between left fielder and center fielder.

8. Backing up on a fly ball, then coming in to make a throw after the catch.
9. Line-drive drill.
10. Picking up a ball by the fence and hitting relay man.
11. Diving catches.

PITCHERS

1. Covering first on anything hit to his left.
2. Backing up first on 6-4-3 double play.
3. Covering home on a tag play.
4. Backing up third and home (forty-five feet back, if possible).
5. Comeback double plays with shortstop and second baseman covering.
6. Force plays at second and third in bunt situations.
7. Squeeze play.
8. Throws to all bases.
9. Fielding ground balls and line drives near the mound.

TEAM OFFENSIVE DRILLS

If space is available, we will break up into several groups. Pitchers will work on sacrifice and squeeze bunts in one area. Infielders may be simulating batters where the next two pitchers are warming up. Certain individuals may be working on a specific drill for correcting hitting faults.

Once the hitter has his swing grooved, we use live pitching with our pitchers throwing from three-quarters to full speed and mixing their pitches. We like the hitter to see the type of pitching he is going to face in a game. Very little is accomplished by lobbing the ball over to a hitter standing there with his shirt unbuttoned who swings all-out at pitching that he will never see in a game.

Intrasquad games are fun. You can have them whenever feasible, with two players doing the managing. There are several ways to control the scrimmage. We have one which we call "one pitch." The pitcher delivers; if the batter hits a fair ball, he runs it out just as in a game. If the batter takes a pitch and it is a strike or if he foul tips, he is out. If the pitch is a ball, he gets a walk. This makes for a speedy game and helps

1

2

3

4

5

6

7

8

9

10

Coach Dick Howser of the New York Yankees demonstrating his bat-speed drill. This is one of the finest ways to increase your bat speed, expecially if you do this with a 55- or 60-ounce lead bat. A college or pro hitter will have a hard time doing this drill, all-out, 150 times. Start your swing as in the first four photos, launching the bat through as quickly as possible. You take your full swing and follow through, as in photos 6 and 7. Your follow-through is held for a split second in photo 7, then, as you see in the next picture, start your swing backwards and fire the bat as hard and quick as you can—like running a movie film camera backwards. In the last two photos, the bat returns all the way along the same path to your original starting position, as in photo 1. Repeat the drill immediately. Young players start with about 20 repetitions, then add 5 to 10 each time until you reach 100 or more. The key to this drill is to go all-out when swinging through and bringing the bat backwards. You will be amazed after a month or two of doing this how much faster you become with your hands and bat.

The bench drill is a real winner for agility and leg development. This drill should be done for about six minutes. (You will have to gradually work up to this—start with three minutes.) The bench can be up to knee height. After a few minutes, you should face the other way and use the opposite leg to hop up to the bench. This is a great conditioner for pitchers' legs and helps pitchers develop the muscles in the leg which gives the push off the rubber.

Pitcher flexibility test for curve-ball pitchers. If you can't bend your hand straight down from the wrist as shown in this picture, you are going to have trouble developing an outstanding curve ball. Some young players don't even realize this and wonder why they never develop the great curve ball. If you lack this flexibility, work with the leaded baseball. If it doesn't improve, you should seriously think about developing a slider, fast curve, or another type of breaking ball.

the players who like to take a lot of pitches. You can also specify three balls as a walk and two strikes for a strike-out.

Each team gets nine outs before changing sides. This saves time and makes for a fast-paced scrimmage.

Other team drills we like are three bunts (against a live defense)—two sacrifice and one squeeze. If the hitter executes all three properly, he gets three additional cuts after bunting. If he misses all three, he gets no swings. If he misses one, he gets two swings. If he fails two, he gets only one swing. This drill has helped improve our bunting.

The following routine is recommended as once-a-week drill, as it is too time-consuming to run every day. The hitter must execute the following facing a live defense and pitching: sacrifice bunt, hit-and-run, moving runner on second over to third by hitting ball on right side, squeeze bunt, and getting ball out of infield.

If the hitter executes these five skills, he gets ten swings. For each of the five he does not execute, he loses two swings. This helps our hitters concentrate hard on each task.

Our one-swing drills also provide fun and benefit. They are all done against a pitcher and defense, with the hitter staying up as long as he produces what is expected:

1. Chokes up and protects the plate with 0-2 count, swinging at anything close.
2. Swings only if he gets pitch in his "joy" zone with 2-0 count.
3. Gets a base hit with one swing.
4. Tries to hit ball on the ground.
5. Squeeze drill—suicide and safety squeeze.

BASE RUNNING DRILLS

1. Each man is timed around the bases, starting with one foot on the plate. Five seconds are added for each base missed, and the bases must be rerun. An excellent time is between 13.2 and 14.5 seconds. The competitiveness of this drill extracts a maximum effort from every player. They enjoy the challenge and the comparisons of times.
2. Going from first to third on balls hit to the outfield.
3. Scoring from second on a hit to the outfield.
4. Getting a big lead at first and watching left-

and right-handed pick-off moves to first.
5. Scoring from third on any ground ball not hit back to the pitcher.
6. Stealing home. We feel that a runner on third should be able to steal home on any pitcher who takes four seconds or longer to deliver the ball to the plate from the start of the windup.
7. Line-drive drill: restrain the natural reaction to go forward.
8. Drawing throws from the outfielders by rounding first hard on base hits to the outfield, tagging up on fly balls, and bluffing to draw throw.
9. Sliding, with emphasis on throws which draw the first baseman off the bag, and slides at the plate.

TEAM DEFENSIVE DRILLS

1. Bunt defense with runner on first, runners on first and second, and squeeze defense.
2. Double cut-offs on balls hit into the outfield alleys.
3. First and third drill: delayed steal, runner on first breaks as catcher cocks arm to return ball to pitcher; bush steal, runner on first breaks as pitcher comes set; and straight steal.
4. Situation drill: any situation can be set up and the ball then fungoed to the desired spot.
5. Call drill: emphasis on pop ups between infield and outfield.

CONDITIONING DRILLS

1. Burma Road—one of the best conditioning drills. The players sprint to first, then form a single line and walk around the bases. When the first man in the line touches home, the players sprint to second and walk home. At the next touch of the plate, they sprint to third and then walk home. At the next touch they sprint around all the bases twice. The teams can be broken up into groups by position to inject more competitiveness into the drill.
2. Foul line to foul line: the players sprint one way and walk the other thirty times.

There is an old saying that "practice makes perfect." But it works only if you practice the right thing.

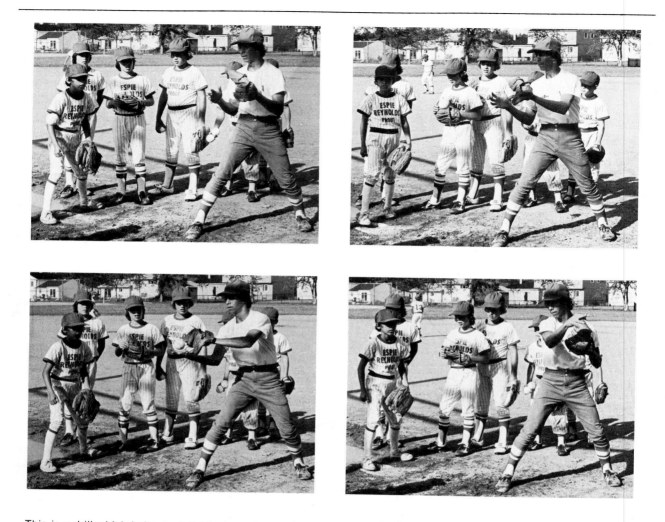

This is a drill which helps an infielder learn to get rid of the ball fast by using the back of his glove as a deflector. In picture 3, he deflects the ball with his glove to his bare hand and, in photo 4, throws into the backstop. Another ball will be fed immediately. As you get quicker with your hands, have the feeder increase the speed with which he feeds the balls. Twenty balls at one time is enough. Go all out with your hands.

20

Hot-Box Situations

There's nothing like a well-executed pick-off or cut-off play to give a team a lift. It's the kind of play that can kill a potentially big inning or rally and save or turn around a ball game.

Conversely, there's nothing more discouraging than to catch a runner and then botch the play, permitting the trapped man to get back safely or, worse, advance a base through a dropped throw, being hit by the ball, or a fielder's obstruction. One major league manager once spent a great deal of spring training time teaching runners in hot-box situations to deliberately run into an infielder as soon as he made a throw.

We begin our hot-box practice early in the year and continue working on it throughout the season. We have our entire squad work on the play so everybody will know how to handle it both offensively and defensively.

In executing the play, we observe the following rules:

1. Try to get the runner with as few throws as possible.
2. When you get the ball, grip it bare-handed in an overhand position, ready to throw.
3. In preparing to receive a throw, stand in the infield side of the base line to reduce the possibility of the throw hitting the runner.
4. Immediately after throwing, veer out of the base line in order to prevent obstruction. Then back up the man you threw to.
5. Don't use voice signals. When you want the ball and can make the tag, take two steps toward the runner. This should be the signal for your teammate to throw to you.
6. In making the tag—with either hand—give with the runner in the direction in which he's moving. This helps eliminate the possi-

1

2

3

4

5

6

Craig Kusik starts the play by catching a runner between first and second. He gives a short toss to Roy Smalley and veers to the outside so the base runner can't run into him and get an interference call. Smalley sets off at full speed and tries to make the tag without another throw. Seeing he won't catch the runner in time (photo 4), he raises the ball high so it is easy to see. Also notice no faking action with his wrist or forearm, just a nice soft toss which is easy for the pitcher to handle and make the tag.

7

8

bility of his knocking the ball out of your hand.

7. When there's more than one base runner, go after one and make the tag as quickly as possible to prevent the other runner(s) from advancing.

8. If you feel that an overhand throw will hit the runner, step to the side and throw side-arm.

9. Remember, you cannot block the base path without the ball (this is obstruction), and if two runners are on the same base, it belongs to the lead runner.

10. If you're the front man in the hot box and have the ball, run hard at the runner to force him back toward his original base.

11. After a successful pick-off at first, the short-stop, who's moving toward the runner in a direct line with the first baseman, should be the lead man. The second baseman should cover second, backing up the shortstop.

Whenever possible, we want our players to stand about three or four feet in front of the bag. This is an advantage on a late throw. If the tag must be made at the base, our man will still have a chance to make the play. If he were farther away, the late throw would cost him the put-out. It's vital to stay out of the runner's way when someone else has the ball.

We don't go for excessive arm-and-ball faking. It can fool the other infielders just as readily as the runner. If you must fake, we suggest using only one motion, to let the receiver know that he'll get the ball on the next motion. The throw should, incidentally, be soft.

The following plays are excellent for setting up hot-box situations:

1. Runners on first and third—pitcher bluffs a pick-off move to third, wheels, and fires to first to trap the runner.

2. In an obvious bunt situation (runners on first and second) or with the runner on first representing an important run, call for a curve ball on the first-base side of the plate. The first baseman charges hard and the second baseman sneaks in behind the runner at first for a pick-off throw from the catcher.

3. With the pick-off in order at second, the catcher comes out in front of the plate and raises his hand or talks it up. This initiates the play. When the catcher squats for his signs, he touches his left shin guard with his bare hand to inform the shortstop to cover. The pitcher checks the runner and looks at the catcher. When the catcher feels the runner is vulnerable, he throws both hands open quickly and the pitcher turns and fires to second.

21
Conditioning and Training: Larry Starr, Cincinnati Reds Trainer

How should a youngster train for prevention of injuries?

Well, first of all, I think, there is not just one program or one particular tool or one mechanical apparatus that can do it. It has to be a comprehensive program of a number of things. A baseball player's main concern should be flexibility. To get or increase flexibility, it is necessary to do stretching-type exercises. The second area of concern is strength. You should include some type of weight training in your program. We at the Cincinnati Reds follow the Nautilus program. The Universal Gym or barbells are also useful. The third area pertains to the throwing arm. It is important that you keep that arm loose, stretched out, and flexible, so we have all our people throw yearround. The fourth area is your heart and lungs—try to develop your cardiorespiratory endurance and so forth. We would ask that you do long-

distance and sprint running. The long-distance running builds endurance; the sprints are important for muscular strength and running skill. Therefore it takes a comprehensive program of flexibility exercises, strength training, throwing, and running. This combination will get you as an individual into the type of physical condition needed to play the game the way it should be played.

What kind of exercises would a person do for the various positions—such as catching, pitching, infield, or outfield—or are there any differences?

Yes, I think there are some differences. One thing to remember is that strength and conditioning are general and skill is specific, so it is important that you work on your entire body. Just because you're a pitcher doesn't mean that you don't need strong legs. If you're a hitter, it doesn't mean that you shouldn't have a good, strong arm. Now one thing that is important to me is that a youngster should not worry too much about specializing in different positions. I don't think a youngster should concentrate all his time on baseball.

What about youngsters at the age of 15 or 16 years, or even 19 years old?

Not even at that age. It is still a game at that time—you should experiment with different things. But, at that age, if you really want a complete comprehensive conditioning program, there is not one area that you should leave out or do more. As you get older, if you're an outfielder, you will probably concentrate a little more on your strength. If you're a pitcher, you are going to concentrate a little more on your flexibility. That is all-important, but the main objective is to do everything.

What things should a youngster avoid to prevent permanent injury or the shortening of a career before it even starts?

Once he is in top physical condition, there are a number of things during the season or at other times that he should do to protect himself and prevent injuries. Of course, the first is proper warm-up. You should never walk on that field without gradually loosening and building up your arm. A pitcher should definitely go out on the mound fifteen or twenty minutes before game time and practice his entire repertoire of pitches. He should throw as hard in the bullpen as he is going to throw during the game. He shouldn't just go halfway in the bullpen, then go out on the mound and pitch as hard as possible.

Another important thing is to always keep the arm warm. On cool or windy days, or even in your room, try to avoid drafts. We always suggest to all our pitchers that they wear a jacket during the game when they are not pitching, of course, and when they are sitting on the bench after the game. If they are back in their room, we ask them to wear a shirt. Keep that arm covered and avoid drafts on the arm, including air-conditioning.

Proper intake of fluids also prevents injury. We always allow our players to drink fluids as they desire. When working out and playing, you sweat—your system loses fluids and salts that must be replaced. So drink as much fluid as you can, and salt your food to replace the salt you lose when you perspire.

Those three areas—proper warm-up, keeping the arm covered, and proper fluid and salt intake—are all-important to a pitcher.

What is your thinking about pitching curve balls, knuckle balls, etc.?

I think that is a very individual question because every person matures at a different age. It depends on the different individual—how quickly he has matured, how his muscular structure has developed, and so forth. But I would say that I advise avoiding curve balls until a youngster is sixteen or seventeen years old. At that time he can work on curves. In the meantime, he can practice his control, velocity, and proper throwing mechanics. At sixteen or seventeen years of age, he is usually physically and mentally mature enough to capably handle something like a curve ball. If he does it too soon and injures the arm, it could be a permanent thing. It could even progress to the point where he could never be able to throw like he used to again. So it is important to protect the young pitcher and not ask him to throw all the breaking pitches until he is physically mature.

How would a person train to avoid injuries such as groin muscle pulls, hamstrings, and so forth?

Again, you get back to the same basic question—getting into proper physical condition to make sure your body is flexible. There are certain individuals who have very tight muscular systems and tight joints. If you are that particular type of individual, then you might have to work harder to increase your flexibility. Another particular individual might have good flexibility but lack good strength. He should work on his strength. It is very important that an individual is strong in his complete system, not just in one particular area. Total body conditioning, with concentration in your particular specialized area, is the desired training program to help master the art of playing baseball.

CINCINNATI REDS BASEBALL STRENGTH TRAINING PROGRAM

Many misconceptions and fallacies have been established concerning weight-training principles and objectives. Often weight training is solely related to the muscle-bound individual who is unable to perform naturally. This is not the case with this program and is definitely not the objective of a baseball strength-training program. On the contrary, besides increasing muscular strength and endurance, you will also show increased joint flexibility and range of motion.

If all other aspects are equal—body proportions, neurological efficiency, cardiovascular ability, and skill—the stronger athlete will win. Absolutely nothing can be done to improve either body proportions or neurological efficiency; however, we can do something about the other factors. Skill is improved by the various drills, as well as the actual playing of the game. Cardiovascular ability is increased through the conditioning program, running, and playing. Muscular strength can also be increased through a conscientious, properly executed strength-training program.

Strength is important in every sport, including baseball. Although some sports may require higher levels, all baseball activities require some degree of strength. Strength is important to the baseball player because it increases the prevention of injury; muscular endurance, thus enabling the player to compete for a longer duration without fatigue; the length of a player's career.

Knowing these important and necessary aspects of muscular strength in baseball, you then must decide on the best method of producing the desired results. You actually have four alternatives, listed in order of best productivity:

1. *Nautilus time machine:* best method for producing full-range, high-intensity, short-duration strength-training exercise. Nautilus is the only rotary form of automatic pre-stretching and full muscular contraction.
2. *Barbells and dumbbells:* limited in full-range exercise but can be beneficial in producing increased strength.
3. *Universal gym machine:* less productive than Nautilus or barbells, but can give some results for strength training.
4. *Iso-kinetic (Mini-Gym, Exergenie, etc.):* does not provide a full-range exercise. This type of exercise equipment should be totally avoided.

Above and next page: Running with a purpose, stretching exercises for flexibility, and getting loose are well illustrated here. Note the different methods—one Twins player is using a bat. Rod Carew in the middle has splendid flexibility.

Based on a review of the available literature, personal communication with leading sports-medicine people, and actual strength-training programs, we have concluded that Nautilus is the best method for developing strength, endurance, and increased flexibility.

When establishing a strength-training program, it must be remembered that strength is general, not specific. You should work all joints throughout their complete line of action. It must also be remembered that many injuries are caused by an improper balance between agonists (muscles which move a body part) and antagonists (muscles which oppose that movement). For example, when strengthening the thigh muscles, if we devoted all our time to the quadriceps and ignored the hamstrings, the ultimate result would be numerous injuries to the hamstrings. This would be true for hips, back, shoulders, elbows, and ankles. Keeping in mind these principles and the specific actions and activities necessary in the game of baseball, the following programs should be instituted:

When doing the program, start out with a relatively light weight, so that you are sure to properly execute the exercise. Lifting a weight is not enough, regardless of the amount of weight. How you lift a weight is a factor of far greater importance. You should be able to do at least eight good repetitions—if you cannot, the weight is too heavy. If you can do twelve or more, the weight is too light and you should add another plate of five or ten more pounds. The program should stress complete range of motion, attempting to obtain a stretch before executing the movement.

Your off-season conditioning program should start two to five weeks after the season ends. During this period, concentrate on individual weaknesses and developing strength throughout the entire body. Depending on the type of equipment, you should be working on all twelve muscular areas as listed previously. Do your strength training on an every-other-day basis, thus allowing your muscles enough time to recover from the work. You should be able to

Muscle Exercised	*Nautilus Time Machines*	*Barbells and Dumbbells*	*Universal Gym Station*
Lower back, hips buttocks	Hip and Back Buo-Poly Contractile Machine	Hip flexor, using high bar	Leg press and hip flexor
Quads	Leg extension	Squats, knee extension	Thigh and knee station
Hamstring	Leg curl	Squats, knee flexion	Knee station
Calves	Calf raises (Multi-exerciser)	Calf raises—barbell on shoulders	Calf raises, shoulder-press station on shoulder
Upper torso	Super pullover	Bench pullover	High lat. station
Latissimus	Behind the neck	Bench pullover	High lat. station
Pectoral muscles	Double chest	Bench press and pectoral lift—on back, arm extended, and lift	Chest-press station
Deltoids Supraspin	Double shoulder	Abduction lift—arm straight at side, lift to shoulder level, and return	Shoulder-press station
Rhomboids Rotators	Rowing machine	Rhomboid lift—lying on stomach, arm straight, lift up, and return	Rowing station
Biceps	Bicep curls	Bicep curls	Bicep curl station
Triceps	Tricep curls	Tricep extension—barbell behind head, arm bent, straighten, and return	Negative dips on dip station
Wrists & Forearms	Wrist curls (Multi-exerciser)	Wrist curls	Wrist curls (bicep st.), wrist developer station

complete the program in approximately one hour or less. Concentrate on form, gradually increasing the resistance as the repetitions become easier. Base your increases on the eight to twelve system as explained previously.

The objectives of the strength-training program are to increase muscular strength and endurance, joint flexibility, muscular speed.

With these objectives in mind, you should keep the following fundamentals when completing *each* repetition:

1. Do all repetitions throughout complete range of motion.
2. Do all repetitions by raising on a 1-2 count, and lowering on a 1-2-3-4 count.
3. Do all repetitions slowly, making sure to pause briefly at the fully contracted and starting positions.
4. Do all repetitions concentrating on form; weight increases will follow accordingly.

1

4

Vern Ruhle, Houston Astros pitcher, starts his stretching routine a half hour before picking up a baseball. Notice in this great sequence study how he stretches all the large and major muscles in his body before touching the ball. The legs, hamstrings, calves, all the way down to his toes; then his middle body, stomach, arms, shoulders, head, and neck. This is the proper way to prepare before throwing. It increases flexibility and cuts down the chance of straining a muscle.

7

8

9

2

5

6

10

11

12

13

20

15

16

1

18

19

22

23

26

29

24

27

28

30

22

Coaching Signs and Signals

DICK HOWSER, NEW YORK YANKEES

Signs originate from the manager in the dugout and are relayed to the third base coach. With the sunken dugouts, most of the signs must be relayed from the waist up. Touching the throat might be the bunt, cap—take off, nose—hit-and-run, ears—squeeze, and chest—steal.

Then, your work as a third-base coach starts. Nothing will be on until you touch an indicator. Say the belt is the indicator. The first thing I touch after the belt will be the sign. We might use left leg—steal, right leg—hit-and-run, left chest—bunt, right chest—squeeze, cap—take. Skin on skin will take off any sign.

The easy way to change your signs is to change your take off or indicator. Another way is to go back to the indicator after you've given a sign which will lock it in.

A big key to coaching third base is *never* get someone thrown out at home plate with no one out.

You always try to get the tempo of a game while coaching. If your opponent has a tough pitcher going, you better think about bunting early and taking a few chances, because you may not get many runs.

EDDIE YOST ON SIGNALS

A good third base coach uses both hands, if possible, simultaneously. The men taking the signs naturally have to know which hand counts. That is, if you say the left hand is the one to concentrate on, that will be the one giving the signs. The guy receiving the signs must concentrate on the hand that counts.

173

1

2

3

7

8

9

13

14

15

4

5

6

10

11

16

The language of the coaching box. Dick Howser illustrates the indicator system. The belt buckle touched with either hand is the indicator that the first sign after will be the signal. (You may change this and make it the second or third sign after the key; you also may change the indicator.)

In the first six photos, there is no sign on as Dick hasn't gone to his belt buckle. In photo 7, he touches his belt buckle, the indicator. The next sign should be the real sign, but in photo 8 he goes to his face with his finger, which is the take-off sign. Thus, all signs are off until he hits the indicator again. In photo 11 he touches the buckle again, putting a sign on. In photo 13 he touches his cap, which puts the hit and run on. In photo 15, Howser touches his buckle, the indicator again, and goes across the letters in photo 16 to put the steal on. The other signs after this are decoys.

17 18 19

20 21 22

COACHING SIGNS AND SIGNALS

The key to signs for young ballplayers is to make them simple and yet at the same time hard for the other team to pick up. You may have the most beautiful set of signs in the world, but if your players are missing them a lot, they are probably too complicated.

Let's take your signs as a coach first. There are indicator, flash, count, and voice or movement signs. Voice signs are excellent for young players, especially if you are a holler type coach. The only drawback to voice signs is that with a large or noisy crowd they may not be heard.

For years at the high school, American Le-

gion, and even college level, I used a voice sign for our squeeze play, and the other team was never able to pick it up. I simply hollered up, "Ducks on the pond," which meant the squeeze play was on the next pitch. We like to have our players answer, so we know everyone has the sign on the squeeze play. We want the hitter to dig his back foot in the dirt or open and close his hands on the bat. The runner on third answers by simply standing on third base with both feet. This becomes very important on this play at the plate or when stealing home. Otherwise the runner may end up with his head in his hands if the hitter misses the sign and is swinging away on either of these plays.

You may want to use a movement sign when you as a coach are not allowed to coach from third base, but must work from the bench or dugout as required in some youth leagues. A great sign for the squeeze play is anytime you leave the bench or dugout and come onto the playing part of the field, the squeeze play will be on the next pitch. You may have a hard time getting your players to understand that even if you argue wih the umpire or talk to the on-deck hitter this is the sign. Once they get this sign, it is very effective under all circumstances.

Voice and movement signs should be part of your natural movement and baseball talk or hollering. A good steal sign, for example, is, "Make it be good." Any time you use the word *make* in your hollering the steal is on.

Here's a sign for the pick-off play at first base with runners on first and/or first, second, and third, when the first baseman is playing behind the runner. First baseman flips some dirt for the sign. As the pitcher delivers to the plate, the first baseman charges to first base, and the catcher throws to first for pick-off. A curve ball outside to a right-handed hitter is a great pitch on this play.

SIGNALS

1. Signals are a necessary part of game.
   a.) Continual missing of signals is usually coach's or manager's fault.
      1.) Do not use a system which indicates left or right.
      2.) Do not use signals which take too much mental reflection to comprehend.
2. Other causes for missed signals.
   a.) Player did not look at coach.
   b.) Player did not look at right time.
   c.) Coach did not give signal properly.
3. Types of signals.
   a.) Flash signals.
      1.) Are flashed to players, for example, by rubbing pants, touching cap, etc.
   b.) Holding signals.
      1.) Are "held" for some time; for example, clenched fists hands, on knees, etc.
   c.) Block signals.
      1.) Separate body into sections or blocks. Use cap as signal for first

three hitters, shirt for next three, and pants for last three hitters in lineup.
   d.) Combination signals.
      1.) Combination of two acts. One act is the indicator or combination sign; for example, covering the belt buckle. This in itself means nothing. However, when buckle is touched *and* cap is touched, the steal is "on."
   e.) The rub-off signal.
      1.) Takes everything "off." Coach puts hit and run on and then changes mind. He puts on rub-off by taking cap off, rubbing shoulder, with forefinger and thumb touching face.
4. Signals for batters.
   a.) The hit.
   b.) The hit and run.
   c.) The sacrifice bunt.
   d.) The suicide squeeze bunt.
   e.) Hit away.
   f.) The take.
5. Signals for the base runner.
   a.) The steal.
   b.) The delayed steal.
   c.) Run on your own.
6. Defensive signals (coach to players).
   a.) For double steal (runners on first and third).
   b.) The signal.
      1.) Throw through to second base.
      2.) Throw back to pitcher.
      3.) Full bluff throw.
   c.) Your sign.
      1.) Rub down on shirt.
      2.) Rub across shirt.
      3.) Fold arms.

CATCHING SIGNS

1. Position for giving signs.
   a.) Squat.
      1.) Right knee points directly at pitcher.
      2.) Right wrist is close to right groin.
      3.) Gloved hand extends over left knee with pocket facing plate.
2. Methods of giving signs.
   (Digit signs used in day games and possibly at night; hand or glove signs used at night.)
   a.) The digit method (using fingers).

1

2

3

4

5

6

7

8

9

10

11

12

13

14

15

16

17

18

Eddie Yost giving signs from third base. In photo 2, he's got the sign from the manager (the manager relays most of his signs from his waist up because some of the major league dugouts are sunken). Picture 7 looks like the key—left hand on the Boston letters. Now which one will be the sign after that: nose in photo 8, hands in 9, or clapping in 10? Perhaps he's taking the sign off in photo 12 by his right hand rubbing his left sleeve. And we thought Morse code was tough!

1.) One finger for fast ball.

2.) Two fingers for curve.

3.) Flexing one finger for change on fast ball.

4.) Flexing two fingers for change on curve.

5.) With bare hand, show where you would like placement of pitch.

b.) Variations of digit method with runner on second base.

1.) Middle sign; 2-1-2 (fast ball); 1-2-1 (curve)

2.) Indicator sign; 1-1-2 (fast ball); first sign indicates 2-1-2 (curve).

3.) Best two out of three; 1-2-1 (fast ball); 1-2-2 (curve).

4.) Odd and even numbers—odd number fast ball; even number curve; 2-2-1 (fast ball); 2-2-2 (curve).

c.) The hand method.

1.) Flat (fast ball).

2.) Up (curve).

3.) Switch (changes the sign).

d.) Pitchout sign for each method.

e.) The glove method.

1.) Glove extended over knee with back facing third base (fast ball).

2.) Gloved hand flexed over knee (curve).

3.) Switch—changes the sign; touching mask, catcher fakes finger sign.

PICK-OFF PLAYS

Varying pick-off plays is a very important part of your defense. It tends to do several things:

1. Takes you out of a big inning.

2. Keeps your base runners close to the bases; consequently, might eliminate scoring of a run or at least give you a play at the base.

3. Tends to confuse the opposing club to a certain extent.

Pick-off Play at Second Base

1. Shortstop or second baseman puts the play on—with sign which the catcher picks up (by taking glove off).

2. Then catcher places his hand on crotch—(fingers pointing downward).

3. Next, the catcher places his hand flat on right thigh or left thigh. The right thigh indicates to the pitcher that the second baseman will cover the base for the pick-off. The placing of the hand on the left thigh indicates that the shortstop will cover the base.

4. The pitcher "looks" back to second base once, then looks at the catcher.

5. Then the catcher, who is in his catching stance, quickly flips his hands when the second baseman (or shortstop) breaks for second base. This is the signal for the pitcher to wheel and throw to second to whoever is covering.

6. Shortstop or second baseman should break for second when:

a.) Base runner places weight on front foot.

b.) Base runner turns head back toward pitcher.

The Daylight Play

This play put into effect by the shortstop and pitcher. The shortstop must jockey himself back and forth behind the runner on second base. Each time he is going back and forth he is getting a little closer to second base. When a pitcher has finally taken his position on the mound and has come to his set position (hands resting in the belt area and relaxed), he will then look to second base. Should he see that there is daylight between the runner and the shortstop, the pitcher knows that the signal for picking the man off at second is in order. *As soon as the pitcher sees the daylight, he sets his head and says to himself, "One thousand one," and throws to second. The shortstop, who knows there is daylight between himself and the runner, immediately breaks for the bag.*

Catcher Calling Pick-off by Using Finger Signs

This pick-off play is called most times by the catcher, but it also can be called originally by an infielder, who in turn gives the sign to the catcher. The catcher at all times must give the sign to the pitcher to advise him the play is in order.

When the catcher, infielder, or pitcher has determined that a runner is getting too far off any of the bases, then an indicator sign between them is given. This can be a variety of motions (pick ear, touch top of cap, etc.). When the pitcher acknowledges the sign to the catcher, the catcher, depending upon which base the play will go to, uses his finger sign accordingly. He will indicate to the pitcher the following way: one finger, first base; two fingers, second base with second baseman covering; three fingers, second base with shortstop covering; four fingers, third base. Now the pitcher has the sign and knows what base he is going to. Both he and the infielder must watch the catcher's clenched right hand, which is resting on the catcher's right knee. The pitcher, who has come to a set position on the mound, will turn and throw to the proper base when he sees the clenched fist open. The infielder, who also has been watching the clenched fist on the right knee, will also break to the bag as he too sees the clenched fist open.

Pick-off Play at First Base Between First Base and Pitcher

This play is used when an obvious bunt situation is in order, and the first baseman is holding the runner on first. Should a ball be thrown or pitched foul, a good time to call this play is "on the very next pitch." It can be set into action by the first baseman going to the mound and telling the pitcher or it can be called with a sign between them both. The manager can also call this play from the bench.

For example: man on first base and bunt in order. The first baseman is holding the man on; the pitcher comes to the set position, throws a pitch to home plate, and it is a ball or fouled off. On the very next pitch after the sign is given, the first baseman will charge two hard steps and return to first base to put the tag on the runner. The pitcher will have to hold the ball a slight second and give the first baseman time to get back. Just a short hesitation is all that is needed, as most times the runner has taken a big lead off the bag.

SEQUENCE PLAY

There are two possibilities for defensively breaking up a successful bunting situation with men on first and second. With bunt in order, the success of this play will depend upon the pitcher throwing a strike. The play can be set up either between the first baseman and third baseman or by the manager. Use signal or go to mound and tell pitcher.

On the first pitch, just as the pitcher gets set and readies himself to throw, the third baseman breaks in hard (his purpose is to field the bunt), the shortstop goes to third base for the put-out, and second baseman goes to second base for possible play there. The first baseman stays on the bag, and the pitcher covers all bunted balls on the first base slide. Should a ball be bunted extremely hard, there is always the possibility of getting a double play on this play.

The reverse of this play can be done on the opposite side and depends upon who is hitting on the opposing club. For example, should a left-handed hitter or player who knows how to bunt to right side only be up, the first baseman charges in hard for the bunted ball, the second baseman covers first base, the shortstop covers second base, and the third baseman stays at third base. The pitcher's job is to cover the third base side.

With runners on first and second, the play most times goes to the third base side if the opposition is trying to execute the play correctly. This being the case, the defense against this most times is to have the third baseman charge.

These plays are not difficult to execute as long as the pitcher throws strikes. The catcher at all times calls the base the play is to be made to.

TIPS FOR COACHES

1. Pick-off play at second base with bases loaded and 3–2 count on hitter is a great play. It catches many teams by surprise.
2. The keys to pick-off plays are timing and repetitious practice so your players get them down pat.
3. Defensively, have signs for where you want your infielders to play (deep—halfway—in).
4. Have a switch sign for your pitcher so he may change one pitch. (Bare hand across the letters.)
5. Have your team stealing on 3–1, 2–0, or 3–2 counts. This often opens up gaps in the defense and makes the other team think your team is hitting and running a lot more than it is. Also, it will keep you away from the double play.
6. Go over all your signs with the entire team until they become second nature to everyone.

The ultimate in coaching aids. This is a baseball team carved from wood by my father. For many years it was on exhibit at Cooperstown in the Baseball Hall of Fame. Bob Feller said "It was the most unique and finest art work with a baseball theme" he had ever seen.

With this type of team or magnetic board you can actually move your players around and show your players the cut-offs and positioning you want. They will learn it much quicker as a result of seeing the overall picture of what you want, as you talk and move your men to their defensive positions.

23

Coaching Aids

To be an outstanding coach, you must stay abreast of the newest thinking and developments in the game and incorporate them into your teaching and coaching. This shows your players that you are working as hard as you expect them to work. Today there are so many aids to make you a better coach and help get the maximum potential out of your proteges.

Television cameras, 8-mm. stop-action movie film, 35-mm. motorized cameras will give you sequence pictures like the ones in this book. Charts for pitching and hitting and magnetic field boards with model players are good to use in skull sessions and chalk talks. Computer sequence printouts are a very new form of analysis which have been used by the Kansas City Royals with their hitters and pitchers.

A single picture in which action is frozen is still a great way of teaching and learning. Many a major league player has been able to correct a fault simply by seeing a photograph shot by a newspaper man.

Here are some ideas which may help you when viewing films or photographs of your players. We use films so a player can see his own faults and will be more ready to accept the advice of others in the correction of these faults. When a player views his films or compares his films with someone else's, we use a teaching method which compares bad to good, or dos with don'ts. There are things a coach must look for when viewing films:

YOUR HITTING FILMS

1. Look at their feet first.
   a.) Is stride either too long or too short?
   b.) Is front foot planted just seconds before ball is hit?
   c.) Does player commit stride way too soon and become a lunge hitter?

d.) Is player's back foot still planted when he hits the ball?

e.) Does player rotate hips?

2. Then, look at hands and arms.

a.) Does player swing the bat at arm's length?

b.) Does the end of the bat move first or do hands come forward first?

c.) Are arms, hands, and wrist lazy? No snap in swing?

d.) Does player lose motion of the bat before he starts his swing, such as a hitch?

e.) Does player drive forward shoulder into ball or pull away?

3. Watch head.

a.) Does player keep head still when swinging or turn it away before he makes contact with ball?

b.) Is head turned enough to get a good look at all pitches with both eyes?

Using films, you can evaluate many things about a hitter. The most important is bat speed. If the batter has good bat speed, he should be a good hitter and a hitter with power. Listed below are the advantages of a speedy bat:

1. Player can pull the good fast ball.

2. Player can wait longer to start his swing and won't be prone to swing at as many bad pitches.

3. The power he possesses is acquired by fast bat speed.

4. A player with a quick bat will not tend to over-stride or pull away from pitches as readily as a player with a slower bat.

5. A player who has a quick bat has good wrist action, which is the essence of a good power hitter.

CHECKING YOUR PITCHING FILMS

1. Watch his feet first.

a.) Does he over-stride or under-stride? If he lands on his heel, he is over-striding.

b.) Does he cross over or throw across his body? This habit tends to make him a bad fielder and a wild pitcher.

c.) After the ball is delivered, is he in a good fielding position?

d.) When pitching from the stretch, does he lift his leg high and cradle his body?

e.) Also from the stretch, does he swing his leg around to gain more motion? This is bad because it will cause him to unload far too slowly.

2. Watch his arm and body.

a.) Does he follow through and bend his back after delivering the ball? Never allow him to become a straight-up pitcher.

b.) Is your pitcher's arm moving forward quickly or does it have lazy action?

c.) Does he throw all his pitches from the same position?

d.) Can you call his pitches from the film?

e.) From the stretch position, does his arm have as quick action as his legs and body? *Very important.*

3. Check the head.

a.) Does he keep his eyes set on the target, or is his head always in motion before throwing the ball?

b.) From the stretch, see if he always looks at second base one time and then throws. This is a very bad habit to develop because a runner can steal third on him standing up.

c.) Have your pitcher vary his head movements to bases. Look short one time, and then longer the next. Look one time, and then look two or more times.

Films can be very helpful to pitchers. The good fast ball pitchers all have quick arms moving forward. If your pitchers are lazy with that arm and you can tell it by watching your films, then they are not putting out to the best ability on the mound. Pitchers can get into slumps, the same as hitters. Using films, a pitcher can compare his good games to his bad, noticing and correcting his mistakes in a very short time.

Remember that for your pitchers to develop an outstanding curve ball their upper throwing arm must be above shoulder height to get that great breaking ball. Check this in your pictures.

Chalk talks and classroom lectures and discussion should cover all defensive and offensive plays, using magnetic board and players. Discuss the rules, wearing of uniform, signs and signals, and what you expect from your players on and off the field.

If your team plays in northern climates, explain your indoor practice routine and what you want to accomplish. You should go over your calisthenics, weight training and stretching, and what the benefits to your players are.

Positional play on bunt defenses, cut-offs, and relays and double steal defenses can be walked through in the gym. You might want to take your team through this offensive routine in the gym. Start with the bench. Tell your players what to look for. (Have your entire squad sit on the bench when you go over this routine.)

1. Tell players to be alert to all play situations so that they will know what to look for in the way of signs and plays when they step into the batter's box.
2. Tell them to study the pitcher's every *move* to the bases and in delivering the ball to the plate so that they will be prepared to get the proper *jump* to advance a base.
3. Tell them to study the qualifications of all your opponents. Do the outfielders on the opposing team have good throwing arms? Are they right- or left-handed throwers?

All of these things are absolutely necessary in playing top-flight baseball. They break down confusion in the mind of the player and enable him to concentrate on the proper thing at the proper time. Next, take all players to the on-deck circle. Tell them:

1. Know position of men on bases in order to get mask and bat out of way in the event of close play at the plate. Get on first base side of plate so runner can see your signal to stand up or slide. It is important to be in runner's line of vision as crowd noise may make it impossible for a word sign to be heard.
2. Watch pitcher to check on type of stuff he is throwing. Always be on the lookout for any movement or any mannerism by the catcher, pitcher, shortstop, or second baseman that may tip off signs.
3. Be mindful of possible play situations and

ready to take the signs when you get to the batter's box.
4. Know the hitter who follows you.

Next, take your entire squad to the batter's box. Tell them:

1. How many are out? What inning is it? What is the play situation? Is the infield in? Do we have men on first, second, or third base, or on all bases?
2. Am I to bunt, hit and run, push the ball to the right side? Will a fly ball score an important run from third base?
3. With all of the above points in mind, through being alerted to them on the bench, *next, look for the sign.*

Look for the sign from the coach with a glance at the opposite coach first; gradually pick up the sign from the coach designated to give it to you. Do not stare at the coach and then immediately attempt to execute. This is a dead giveaway and permits opponents to steal your signs.

Next, take your entire squad to first base and explain in detail their duties when becoming a base runner.

1. Find the ball. How many are out? Is the pitcher on the rubber? Does he have a good move? (The move of this pitcher should be well in mind because of studying it while on the bench and when waiting for your turn at bat.) Where are the outfielders playing the hitter? Will the ball hit be on his glove hand or throwing hand?
2. Pick up the sign with your foot on the base, with a glance around so that you can see the coach, hitter, and pitcher with no loss of time. Have a uniform set of signs so that all players involved take the signs at the same time.
3. Get your lead off first base (go off facing the pitcher, first putting the left foot behind the right foot, continuing in that motion until a comfortable lead is taken). You should never be off balance with this system.
4. Your first move to second base should be

when the pitcher makes his first move to the batter (watching his front foot is always good). Then, start to second base with a crossover of the left foot. That puts you at full speed quickest.

5. Dash and look over left shoulder to see if ball has been hit. If you are lost on the play, look at your third base coach for directions.

Next, take all players to second base and let them all assume they are base runners. Their instructions:

1. Size up the play situation from the bag. Do not jog back and forth, taking an anxious lead. Have a definite plan in mind.

2. Ask yourself these questions: Does this team have any trick pick-off plays? What kind of a move does this pitcher have? Where are the outfielders playing the hitters? Where are the infielders playing the hitters? What inning is it? Is my run the winning or tying run? *Pick up sign, if any.*

3. Get your lead the same as on first, facing the pitcher, and when the catcher is giving the signs (less apt to attempt pick-off play then).

4. Take a comfortable lead, ready to go either way, depending on whether the ball is hit or missed. Safeguard against going to third base on ball hit to third base side of the shortstop. (You usually are an easy out on that faulty baserunning move.)

5. Go back to second base after every pitch and stand on the bag, facing in a way that you pick up pitcher, catcher, coach, and shortstop, all in the same glance.

Complete circle by taking all players to third base. Tell them:

1. What is the play situation? The inning? How many out? If the infield is playing in, does the coach want me to go home (as the coach, you will tell him if you want him to make the ball go through or attempt to score)?

2. Tag up on all fly balls or line drives to the outfield.

3. Look for sign to go in on double steal. Make sure you have an understanding on the double steal to go in or hold up. With no one out or one out, runner on first always goes through; with two out he holds up.

After you have taken your squad around the bases the first time, start asking them questions so that they realize they definitely are to know this, and it is something you are trying to build in your team—an attitude of being thinking ballplayers.

24

Final Tips for Coaches

1. *Teach fundamentals. This is the backbone of playing great baseball.*
2. Play your nine best players and stick with them.
3. Learn about focusing eye and eye speed in focusing and picking up rotation of ball when pitcher releases it.
4. Have your pitchers run and run and then run some more. Long distance and sprints (one to five miles before practice and wind sprints, foul line to line). Why? Basically, pitchers have their bodies and the baseball to work with. The idea is to get them to put 100 percent of the energy in their bodies into the ball, which creates velocity. It is impossible to use all 100 percent. The unused energy from the wind-up and delivery has to dissipate somewhere. It is absorbed by the body in a recoil action. How that energy, that shock at the end of every pitch is absorbed, determines whether a pitcher will have arm trouble. You want your pitchers to finish their delivery so that the big muscles of the body—the thighs and buttocks—absorb the shock. That's why pitchers run—to strengthen the large, lower body muscles. If your pitcher's legs are weak and he finishes his delivery stiff-legged when he gets tired rather than flexible and bouncy, they will lose their velocity and stuff and your pitcher may end up with a ruined arm. Another telltale mannerism showing a pitcher is getting tired is when his arm starts to drop down just a little bit from his natural release point.
5. Have your battery use multiple signs the whole game. By doing this, your pitcher doesn't have to concentrate on one more thing when he gets into trouble with base runners.
6. Don't criticize player on day that a game is lost.

7. Try praising boy before making a criticism.
8. Don't criticize player without explaining how the play should be made for proper technique.
9. Change player's position during intra-squad games early in the year.
10. Do hard physical conditioning work at the end of practice after early season conditioning. Baseball skills require fantastic hand-eye coordination (hitting-pitching, etc.), and if your players are tired out, there is no way they will be able to do their best.
11. Make use of coach's playbook and your organizational charts and have practice plans for every day (including bad weather days). This will make your players confident and everyone know what they will be doing.
12. Lots of good luck to you with your coaching. As Branch Rickey once said, after all the hard work, design, thinking, and skills, good luck is the residue of what's left over.
13. Have fun coaching and let your players have fun practicing and playing baseball.

25

Infield Practice: Pitching, Hitting, and Organizational Charts

From the majors to the sandlot, this practice is basically the same. Why? Because it includes practice in the execution of practically every play that appears in a game.

Be sure your squad has fifteen minutes to warm up their arms. If you use this practice to finish up a workout on an upbeat, be sure the outfielder is given a chance to charge ground balls and make him move. Don't make fly balls routine. The same goes for infielders; make the plays tough.

Before a game, hit to your outfield first. Don't hurry this; by doing it, you let your outfielders know they are as important as your infielders to the success of your team. They are on exhibition and this is a real motivator in helping them strive for perfection.

If your infield drill is conducted with hustle and pepper, it is a real morale booster. Your infielders will talk to one another. The infielders will throw the ball around the horn and step up the tempo with which the ball is thrown.

If your team has developed this type of spirit, your players over the season will develop an eagerness to do their things with class and spirit.

OUTFIELDERS

Left fielder: two throws to second; three throws to home plate.
Center fielder: two throws to third; three throws to home plate.
Right fielder: two throws to third base; three throws to home plate.

PLANNED INFIELD

You can cut rounds as time limits you or not have catcher throw to covering infielder on each round to save time also.

189

INFIELDERS
(Whoever fields the ball takes the return from the catcher.)

Rounds	Direction of ball	Speed ball is hit	Play procedure
1.	Directly at player	Normal	Throw to first; get one
2.	Hit to second base side of infielder	Normal	Throw to first; get one
3.	Hit to foul line side of infielder	Normal	Throw to first; get one
4.	Hit to second base side of infielder	Hard	Throw to second; get one
5.	Hit to foul line side of infielder	Hard	Throw to second; get one
6.	Directly at player	Easy	Throw to first; get one or first baseman throw to third
7.	Directly at player	Normal	Throw home for tag
8.	Pop flys to catcher		

Infielders

(Whoever fields the ball takes the return from the catcher.)

Roll the ball down both foul lines and out in front of the plate so the catcher gets plenty of practice on throwing bunt plays.

Another way to take infield workout:

1. First round (whoever fields the ball takes the throw from the catcher).
   a.) Straight to third base; throw to first base, back home
   b.) Ball straight to shortstop, first base, home, second base, third base (or home)
   c.) Ball straight to second base, first base, home, second base, third base (or home)
   d.) Ball straight to first base, second base, first base, home, first base, home
   e.) Roll ball down first base line; catcher to first base, second base, third base, home.
2. Second round
   a.) To right of third base, first base, home, third base, second base, first base, home
   b.) To right of shortstop, first base, home, second base, home
   c.) To left of second base, first base, home, second base, third base, or home
   d.) To left of first base, second base, first base (get back!!), home, first base, home
   e.) Roll ball straight toward center for catcher, second base, third base, home
3. Third round
   a.) To left of third base, first base, home, third base, home
   b.) To left of shortstop, first base, home, second base, first base, or home
   c.) To right of second base, first base, home second base, third base or home
   d.) To right of first base, second base, first base, home, first base, home
   e.) Roll ball down third base line for catcher, third base, second base, first base, home, third base, home
4. Double play round.
5. Another double play round
6. Round as first to catcher at home
7. Final round to catcher at home
8. Pop flies to catcher

HITTING CHART
PLAYER'S NAME

1. Draw dotted line—grounder
2. Straight line—fly ball or line drive
3. Put down what batter does. For example:

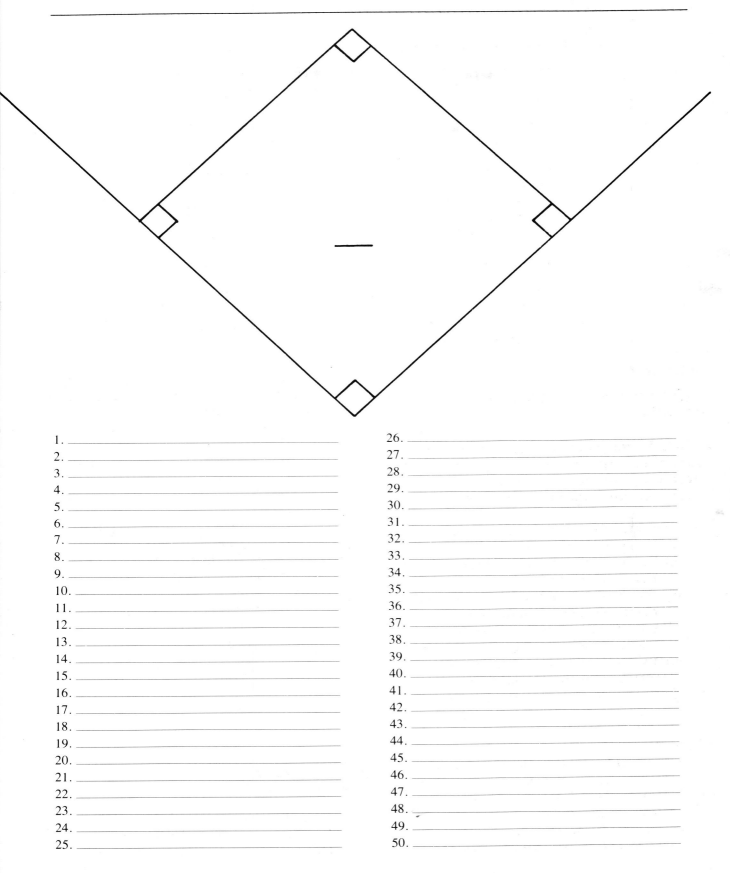

1. _____
2. _____
3. _____
4. _____
5. _____
6. _____
7. _____
8. _____
9. _____
10. _____
11. _____
12. _____
13. _____
14. _____
15. _____
16. _____
17. _____
18. _____
19. _____
20. _____
21. _____
22. _____
23. _____
24. _____
25. _____

26. _____
27. _____
28. _____
29. _____
30. _____
31. _____
32. _____
33. _____
34. _____
35. _____
36. _____
37. _____
38. _____
39. _____
40. _____
41. _____
42. _____
43. _____
44. _____
45. _____
46. _____
47. _____
48. _____
49. _____
50. _____

Coach's Organizational Chart

Opponent _____   Date _____

Pregame Duties

1. Pregame meal at _____. Game starts at _____.
2. Bus leaves at _____ from _____. Be prompt.
3. Report on field by _____ dressed and ready to go.
4. We hit at _____.
5. Batting practice pitchers _____ + _____.
6. Batting practice catcher _____.
7. Infield fungo hitters _____ + _____.
8. Infield fungo shagger _____ + _____.
9. Outfield fungo hitter _____.
10. Outfield fungo shagger _____.
11. Ball shagger for batting practice pitcher _____.
12. Infield practice starts at _____.

Game Duties

1. Catcher to warm up starter _____.
2. Bull pen catcher _____.
3. First base coach _____.
4. Bull pen pitchers
   a. Long man _____.
   b. Short man _____.
5. Scorekeeper _____.
6. Game notes keeper _____.
7. Pitching charts _____.
8. Opponents' pitching charts _____.
9. Reading opponent pitcher _____.
10. Reading coaches' signs _____.

Starting Line-up

1. _____
2. _____
3. _____
4. _____
5. _____
6. _____
7. _____
8. _____
9. _____

✓ —Fast Ball   R   H   E

○ —Curve   Team_____ ____ ____ ____

ᴎ —Change   Versus_____ ____ ____ ____

— —Slider   At_____ Weather_____

S —Screw Ball   Date_____

✕ —Knuckle Ball   Prepared by_____

BATTER

PITCHER		FAST	CURVE	CHANGE	SLIDER	SCREW	KNUCKLE		TOTALS
	STRIKES								
	BALLS								
	STRIKES								
	BALLS								
	STRIKES								
	BALLS								
	STRIKES								
	BALLS								
	STRIKES								
	BALLS								
	STRIKES								
	BALLS								

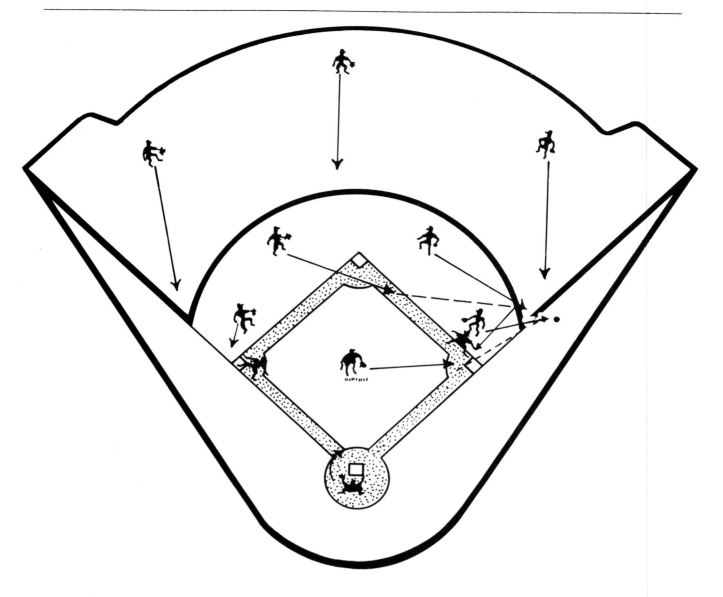

FOUL BALL PLAY (SHORT) WITH RUNNERS ON FIRST AND THIRD—RIGHT FIELD LINE

Pitcher
Cover first base.

Catcher
Cover home plate.

First baseman
Try to catch fly ball.

Second baseman
Try to catch fly ball.

Shortstop
Race to spot (20-30 feet) from second base to become cut-off man.

Third baseman
Cover third base.

Left fielder
Back up third base.

Center fielder
Come in and back up second base.

Right fielder
Come in and back up first base.

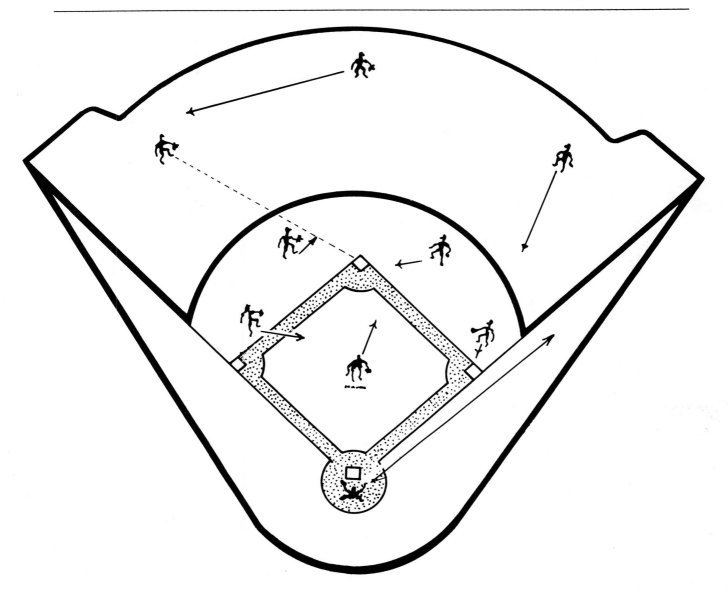

SINGLE TO LEFT FIELD
NO ONE ON BASE

Pitcher
  Back up second base in direct line of throw from left fielder.

Catcher
  Follow runner to first base.

First baseman
  Cover first base.

Second baseman
  Cover second base.

Shortstop
  (Cut-off man) line up ball to second base.

Third baseman
  Move in toward third base area.

Left fielder
  Make hard line throw, head high, to shortstop and to second base on fly if possible.

Center fielder
  Move toward left fielder calling for play at second base.

Right fielder
  Come in and back up first base.

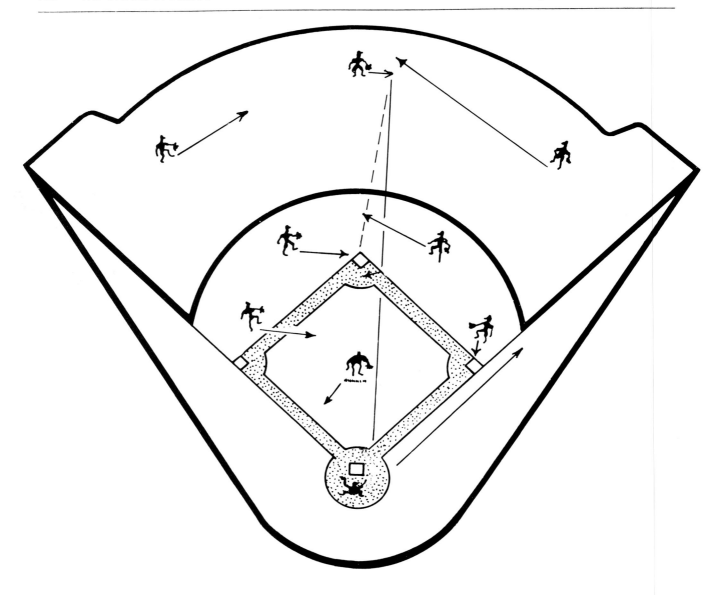

SINGLE TO CENTER FIELD
NO ONE ON BASE

Pitcher

Move to position between home plate and mound in direct line of throw from center fielder (backing up play).

Catcher

Follow runner down first base and line up first base bag with fielder fielding ball.

First baseman

Make sure runner tags the base in making the turn, then cover first base.

Second baseman

Position self as cut-off man between center fielder and second base bag.

Shortstop

Cover second base and prepare to take throw from center fielder in case runner tries to take extra base.

Left fielder

Move toward center fielder and call the play.

Center fielder

Make hard line throw toward cut-off man, head high with enough on it so as to carry to second base bag.

Right fielder

Move toward center field area, backing up play.

Third baseman

Cover third base.

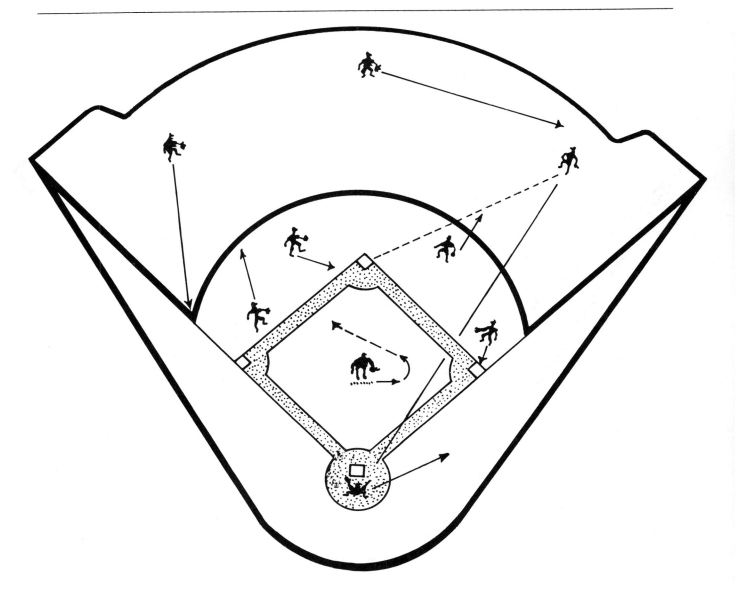

SINGLE TO RIGHT FIELD
NO ONE ON BASE

Pitcher

Break toward first base in case he has to cover first base. After ball passes infield, he then may drift toward short-stop position (helping to back up play).

First baseman

Cover first base and make sure runner tags first base.

Second baseman

He is cut-off man (40-45 feet) from second base in direct line with bag and right fielder.

Shortstop

Cover second base.

Third baseman

Back up shortstop covering second base.

Left fielder

Move in back of third base area.

Center fielder

Move toward right fielder calling the play.

Right fielder

Make low line throw (head high) to cut-off man second base (on fly if possible).

Catcher

Follow runner down and back up first base in line with right fielder.

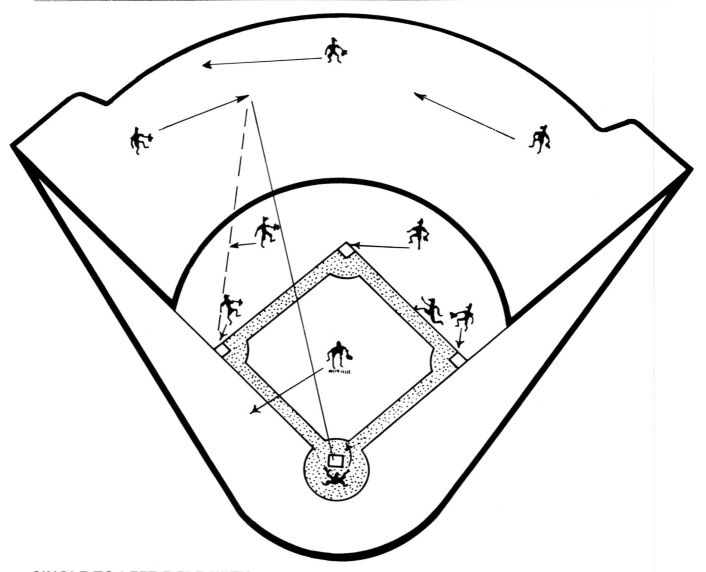

SINGLE TO LEFT FIELD WITH RUNNER ON FIRST BASE

Pitcher
Back up third base in line with throw from left fielder.

Catcher
Protect home plate.

First baseman
Cover first base. Make sure runner tags first base.

Second baseman
Cover second base. Make sure runner tags second base bag.

Shortstop
Position yourself about 40-45 feet from third base on direct line from third base to the outfielder fielding the ball.

Third baseman
Cover third base and prepare for tag.

Left fielder
Anticipate where relay man is (shortstop). Try and hit him head high.

Center fielder
Back up left fielder and let him know what to do.

Right fielder
Move in right center field as back-up man in case of overthrow from relay man.

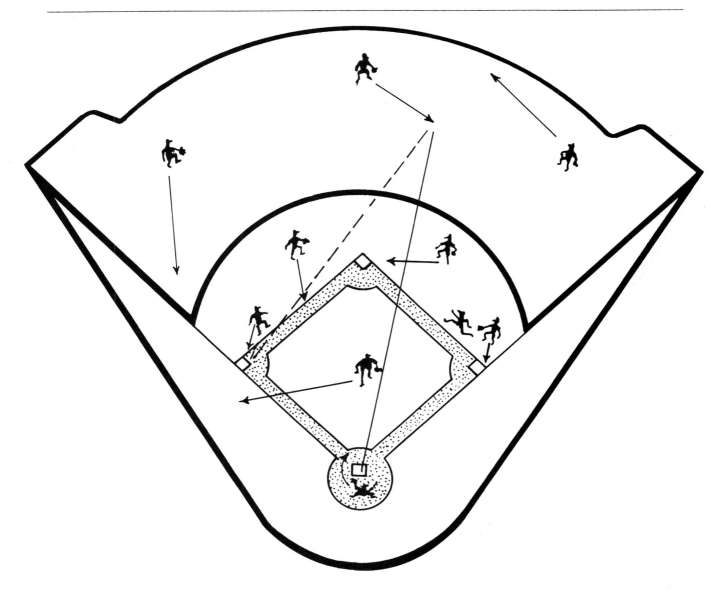

SINGLE TO CENTER (RIGHT) WITH RUNNER ON FIRST BASE

Pitcher

Back up third base in line with throw.

Catcher

Protect home plate.

First baseman

Cover first base. Make sure runner tags first base.

Second baseman

Cover second base. Make sure runner tags second base bag.

Shortstop

Position yourself about 40-45 feet from third base, on a direct line from third base to the outfielder fielding the ball.

Third baseman

Cover third base and prepare for tag.

Left fielder

Move in back of third base area.

Center fielder

Anticipate where relay man is (shortstop). Try and hit him head high.

Right fielder

Move toward ball and let teammate know what to do.

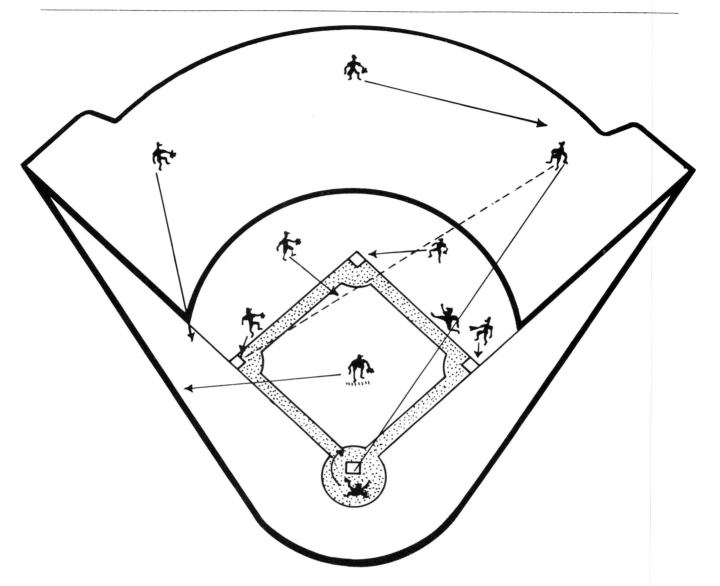

SINGLE TO RIGHT FIELD WITH RUNNER ON FIRST BASE

Pitcher
Back up third base in line with throw.

Catcher
Protect home plate area.

First baseman
Cover first base. Make sure runner tags first base.

Second baseman
Cover second base. Make sure runner tags bag.

Shortstop
Place self about 45 feet from third base, on direct line from third base to the outfielder fielding the ball.

Third baseman
Cover third base.

Left fielder
Move in toward third base area.

Center fielder
Back up right fielder and let him know where to throw ball.

Right fielder
Anticipate where relay man is (plus speed of hit, if chance of play at third base).

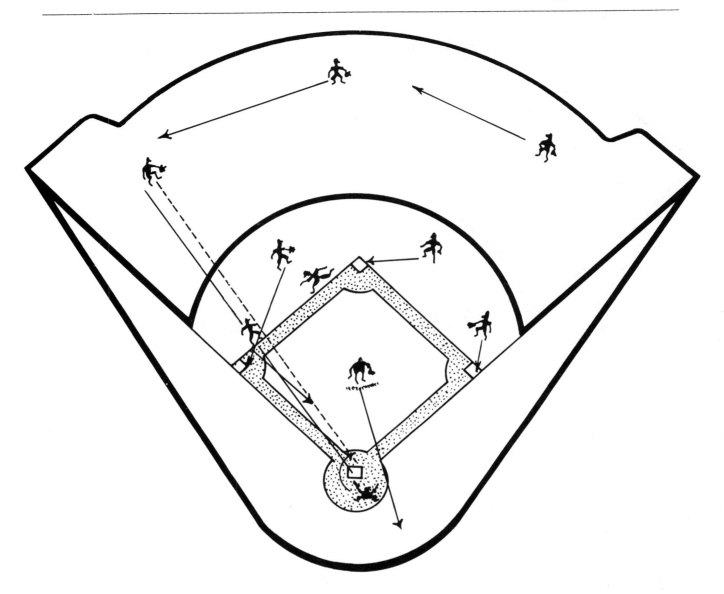

SINGLE TO LEFT FIELD WITH RUNNER ON SECOND BASE AND SCORING

Pitcher

Back up home plate in direct line from outfielder throwing home.

Catcher

Prepare for tag and blocking of plate.

First baseman

Cover first base and make sure runner tags first base.

Second baseman

Cover second base.

Shortstop

Cover third base.

Third baseman

Take position about 40-45 feet from home plate to become cut-off man.

Left fielder

Anticipate where relay man is (third base) and try to hit him head high.

Center fielder

Back up left fielder and let teammate know what to do.

Right fielder

Move in toward right center field, in line of second base in case of overthrow from cut-off man and catcher (possibly).

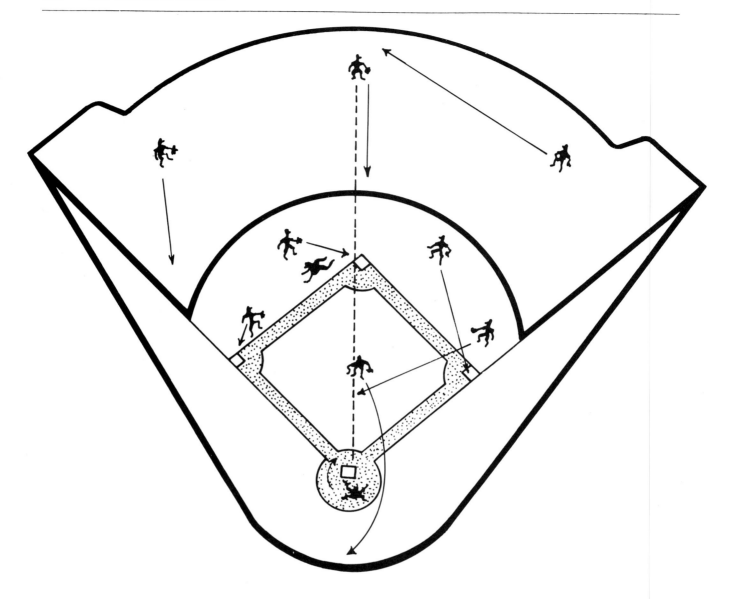

SINGLE TO CENTER WITH RUNNER ON SECOND BASE AND SCORING

Pitcher

Back up home in direct line from outfielder throwing home.

Catcher

Prepare for tag and blocking of plate.

First baseman

Move into position 40-45 feet from home plate in line of throw, to be a cut-off man.

Second baseman

Cover first base.

Shortstop

Cover second base.

Third baseman

Cover third base.

Left fielder

Move in back of third base area.

Center fielder

Anticipate where relay man is (first base). Try and hit him head high.

Right fielder

Move toward ball and let teammate know what to do.

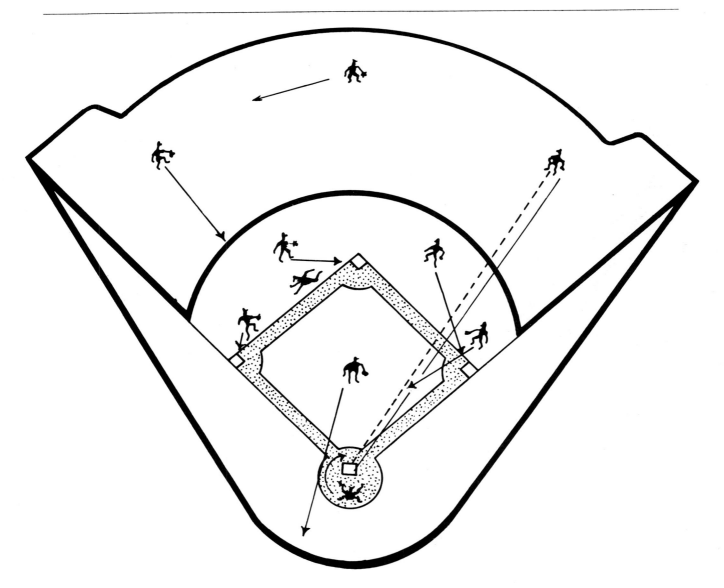

SINGLE TO RIGHT FIELD WITH RUNNER ON SECOND BASE AND SCORING

Pitcher
   Back up home plate in direct line of ball from outfield.

Catcher
   Prepare for tag and blocking of plate.

First baseman
   Take position about 40-45 feet from home plate to become cut-off man.

Second baseman
   Cover first base.

Shortstop
   Cover second base.

Third baseman
   Cover third base.

Left fielder
   Move in back of third base area.

Center fielder
   Move in back of second base area (back-up man) in case of bad throw from catcher or cut-off man.

Right fielder
   Make low, hard throw toward the cut-off man (first base), head high.

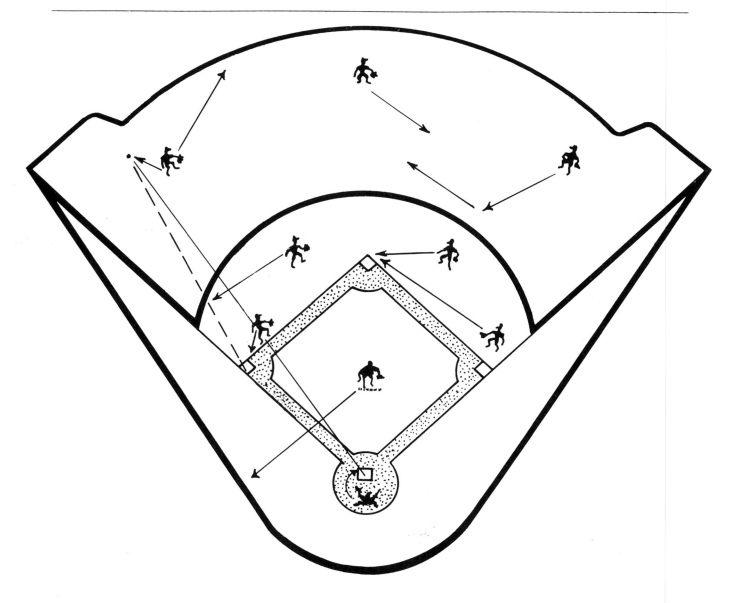

SURE DOUBLE LEFT FIELD LINE NO ONE ON BASE

Pitcher

Back up third base in direct line with throw from outfielder.

Catcher

Cover home plate.

First baseman

Watches runner tag first base; then becomes trailer backing up second base.

Second baseman

Cover second base.

Shortstop

Becomes cut-off man between third base and left fielder.

Third baseman

Cover third base.

Left fielder

Hard line (head high) throw to shortstop.

Center fielder

Moves in left center field and calls play to teammate.

Right fielder

Floats and gets in direct line with throw to second base (in case shortstop makes play).

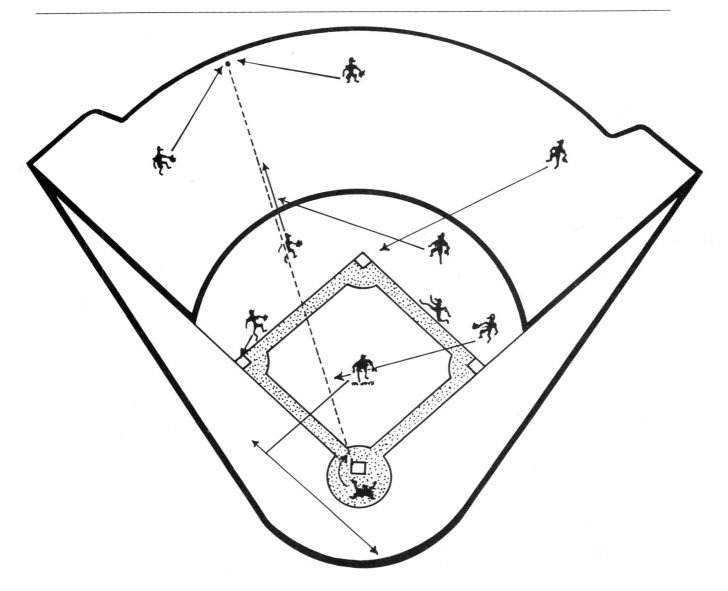

DOUBLE TO LEFT CENTER WITH RUNNER ON FIRST BASE AND SCORING

Pitcher
Become a floater between home and third base and then back up the base where throw is going.

Catcher
Prepare for a play at plate.

First baseman
Position self between mound and third (40-45 feet in front of plate) in direct line with throw from outfielder.

Second baseman
Trail about 30 feet behind shortstop.

Shortstop
Go to spot in left field in direct line with outfielder and plate.

Third baseman
Cover third base.

Center fielder
Back up left fielder; also inform him of play.

Right fielder
Cover second base.

Left fielder
Anticipate next play and position of relay man.

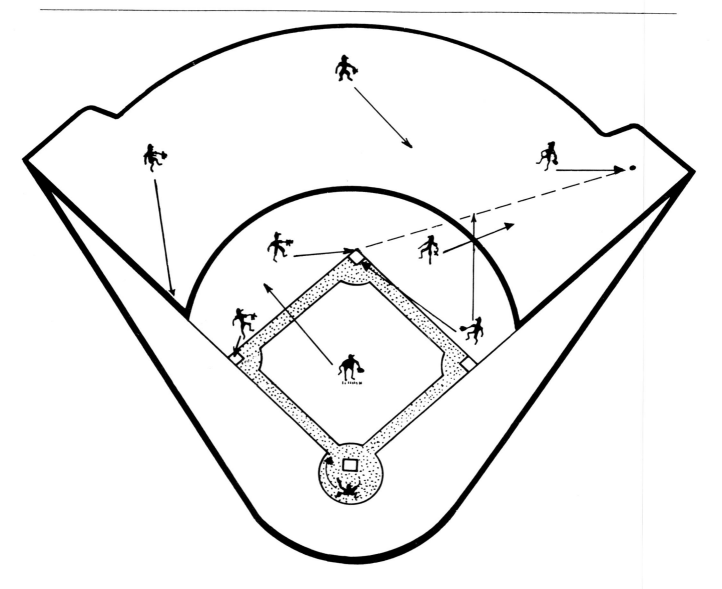

SURE DOUBLE RIGHT FIELD
NO ONE ON BASE

Pitcher
   Back up second base in line of throw in (shortstop) area.

Catcher
   Cover home plate.

First baseman
   Become trailer cut-off man behind second baseman.

Second baseman
   Become first cut-off man in direct line with second base.

Shortstop
   Cover second base.

Third baseman
   Cover third base.

Left fielder
   Back up pitcher (in shortstop area) in line of relay (from second baseman).

Center fielder
   Come in back of second base.

Right fielder
   Make hard line throw to second baseman (first cut-off man) head high.

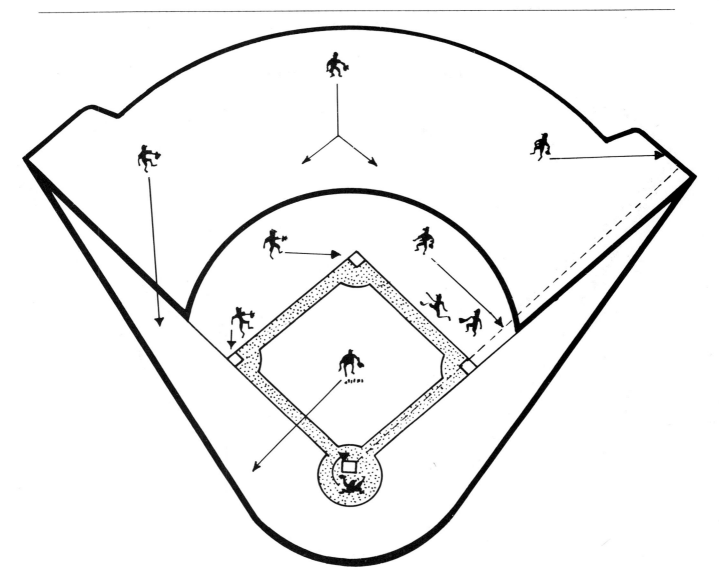

SURE DOUBLE TO RIGHT FIELD LINE WITH RUNNER ON FIRST BASE

Pitcher
 Back up home plate in line with ball.

Catcher
 Cover home plate and prepare for tag play.

First baseman
 Station self 40-45 feet in front of home plate to be cut-off man in line with thrown ball.

Second baseman
 Line up ball with first baseman; is first cut-off man in direct line with plate.

Shortstop
 Cover second base.

Third baseman
 Cover third base.

Left fielder
 Back up third base area.

Center fielder
 Move in right center and call play for teammate.

Right fielder
 Make hard line, head high throw to cut-off man at second base.

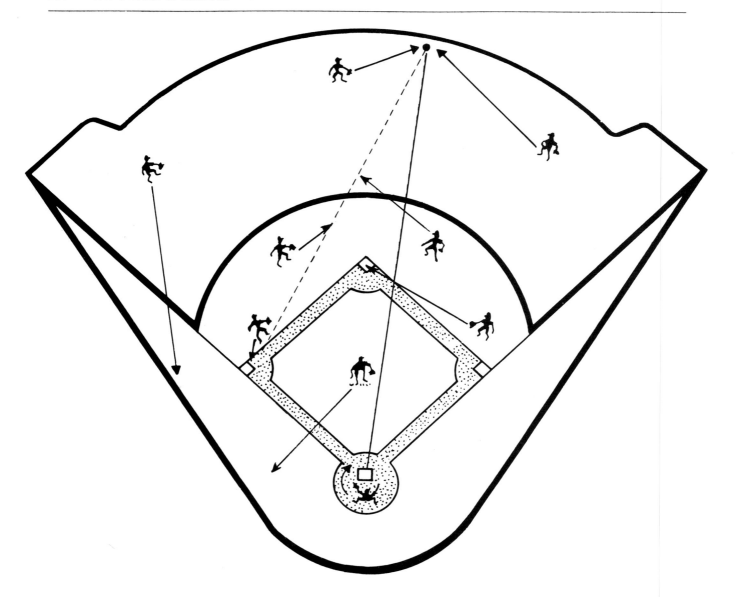

POSSIBLE TRIPLE TO RIGHT CENTER NO ONE ON BASE

Pitcher
   Back up third base.

Catcher
   Cover home plate.

First baseman
   Be sure runner touches base; then cover second base.

Second baseman
   First cut-off man in lining ball up with third base.

Shortstop
   Is trailer behind second baseman.

Third baseman
   Cover third base.

Left fielder
   Move in back of third base area.

Center fielder
   Backs up right fielder and calls play.

Right fielder
   Make hard, low line throw (head high) to second baseman cut-off man.

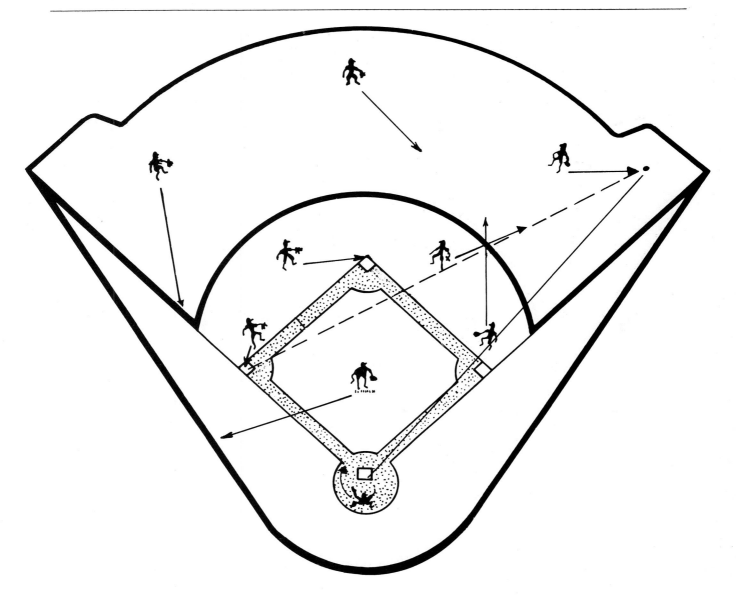

POSSIBLE TRIPLE TO RIGHT FIELD CORNER NO ONE ON BASE

Pitcher
   Back up third base.

Catcher
   Cover home plate.

First baseman
   Back up second baseman (trailer).

Second baseman
   Is first cut-off man in direct line with third base.

Shortstop
   Cover second base.

Third baseman
   Cover third base.

Left fielder
   Move in third base area near foul line.

Center fielder
   Move in back of second base.

Right fielder
   Hard, low line throw (head high) to second baseman, first cut-off man.

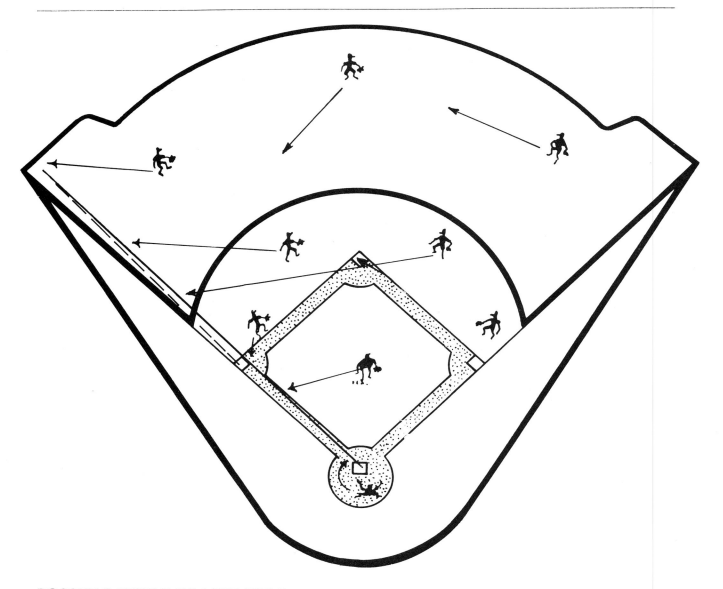

POSSIBLE TRIPLE TO LEFT FIELD CORNER NO ONE ON BASE

Pitcher
   Back up third base in line with plate.

Catcher
   Cover home plate.

First baseman
   Cover second base.

Second baseman
   Become trailer behind shortstop (first cut-off man).

Shortstop
   Be the cut-off man for a possible throw to third base.

Third baseman
   Cover third base and prepare for tag.

Left fielder
   Hard, low line throw (head high) to shortstop.

Center fielder
   Come in left center area.

Right fielder
   Move in back of second base area.

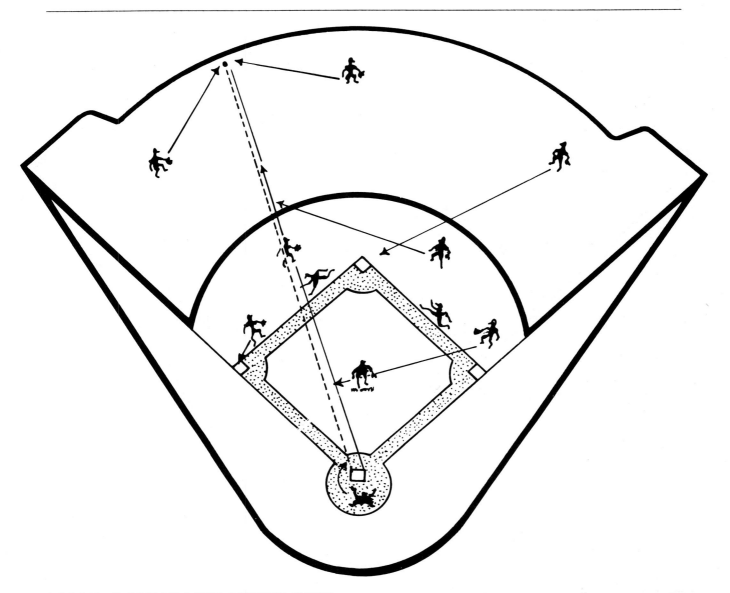

POSSIBLE TRIPLE LEFT CENTER WITH RUNNER ON FIRST BASE AND RUNNER SCORING

Pitcher
Go halfway between home and third base (become a floater) and then back up the base where throw is going.

Catcher
Cover home plate.

First baseman
Move to spot 40-45 feet from home plate in line with throw to be cut-off man.

Second baseman
Back up shortstop (trailer).

Shortstop
Is first cut-off man in lining up play with plate.

Third baseman
Cover third base.

Left fielder
Make hard line throw (head high) to first cut-off man, shortstop.

Center fielder
Back up left fielder and call play.

Right fielder
Cover second base.

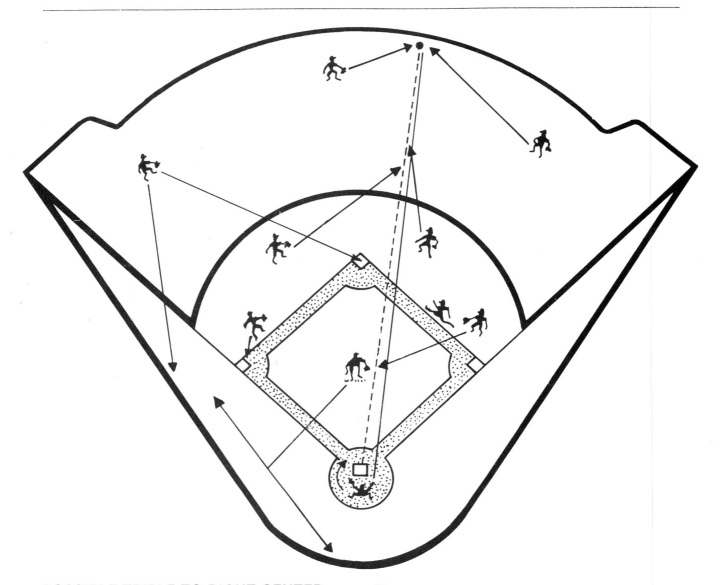

POSSIBLE TRIPLE TO RIGHT CENTER FIELD WITH RUNNER ON FIRST BASE AND SCORING

Pitcher

Go halfway between home and third base and then back up the base where throw is going (a floater).

Catcher

Cover home plate.

First baseman

Move into spot 40-45 feet from home plate in line with throw, to be cut-off man.

Second baseman

Is first cut-off man in lining up play with plate.

Shortstop

Is trailer (cut-off man) behind second baseman.

Third baseman

Cover third base.

Left fielder

Cover second base.

Center fielder

Back up first fielder and call play.

Right fielder

Hard line throw (head high) to first cut-off man, second baseman.

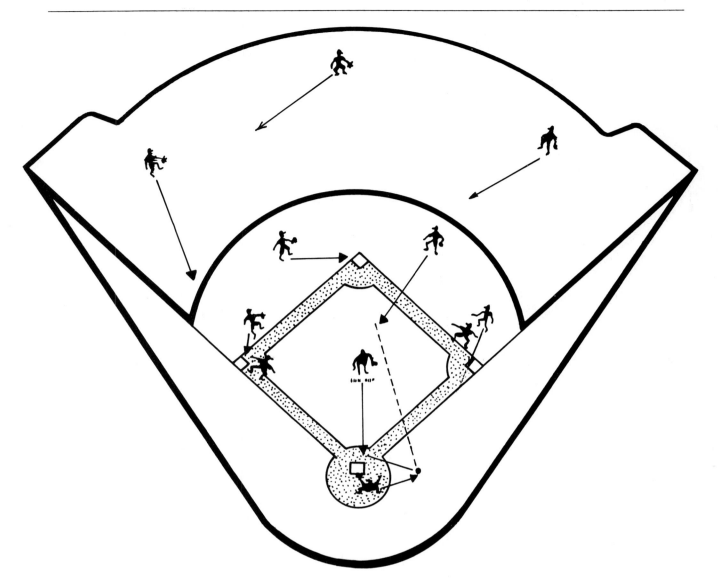

FOUL BALL PLAY WITH RUNNERS ON FIRST AND THIRD NEAR FIRST DUGOUT

Pitcher
  Cover home plate.

Catcher
  Catch foul ball and throw to second baseman as cut-off man.

First baseman
  Cover first base.

Second baseman
  Race to spot near mound for cut-off in line of second base.

Shortstop
  Cover second base.

Third baseman
  Cover third base.

Left fielder
  Come in and back up third base.

Center fielder
  Come in and back up second base.

Right fielder
  Come in and back up first base.

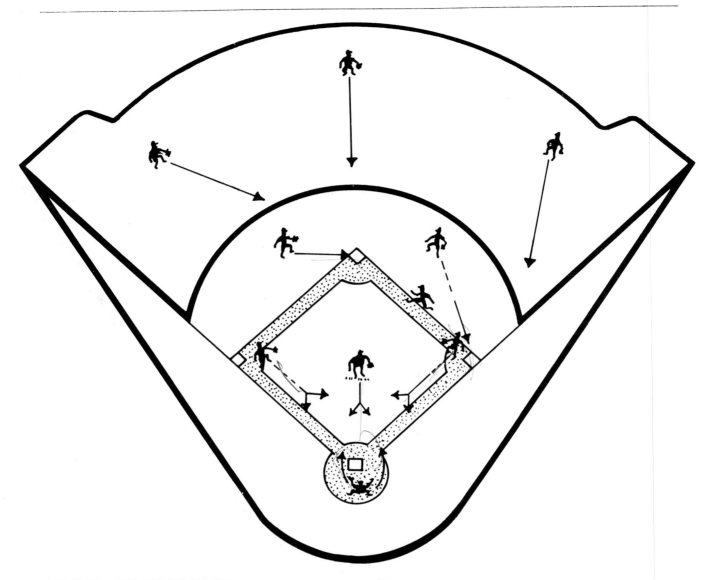

RUNNER ON FIRST BASE (WITH BUNT IN ORDER)

Pitcher
Break toward plate after releasing ball.

Catcher
Field all bunts possible; call the play, cover third base when third baseman fields the bunt in close to home plate.

First baseman
Cover the area between first and the mound.

Second baseman
Cover first base; cheat by shortening position.

Shortstop
Cover second base.

Third baseman
Cover the area between third and the mound.

Left fielder
Move in toward second base area.

Center fielder
Back up second base.

Right fielder
Back up first base.

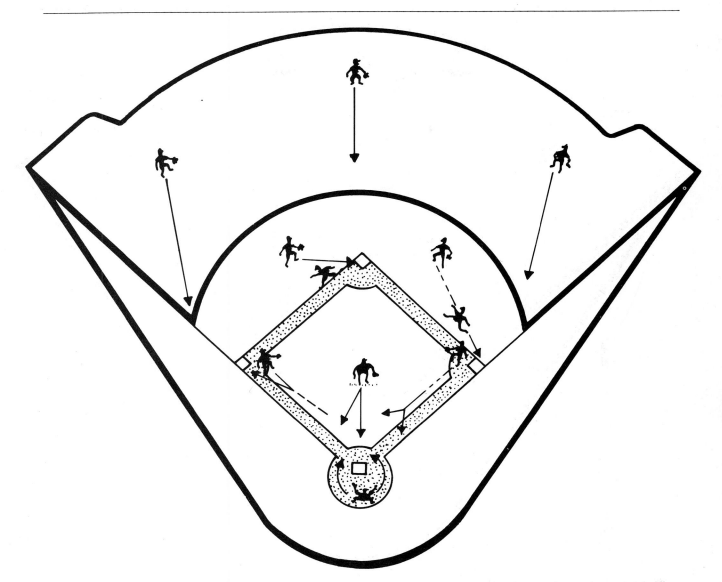

RUNNERS ON FIRST AND SECOND (WITH BUNT IN ORDER)

Pitcher

Break toward third-base line upon delivering the ball.

Catcher

Field bunt in front of plate. Also call the play.

First baseman

Is responsible for all balls in the area of first and direct line from the mound to home.

Second baseman

Cover first base.

Shortstop

Hold runner close to bag (by jockeying before pitch). Cover second base.

Third baseman

Take position on edge of grass approximately 12 feet from third base (at angle where body is facing third so that with peripheral vision you can see bag and bunter at same time). If pitcher yells, you go to bag for put out. If no sound, charge ball and make play to first base; if hard enough, possible play at second base.

Left fielder

Back up third base.

Center fielder

Back up second base.

Right fielder

Back up first base.

POP FLIES TO THE INFIELD

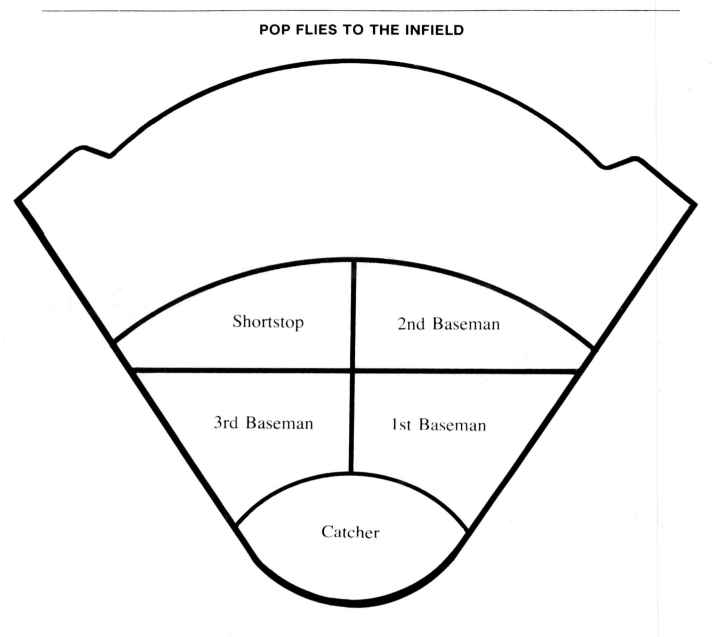

An infield pop fly will be all infielders' responsibility, and they must try for the ball until one fielder takes charge by calling for the play.

a. When calling, yell loudly three or four times. Wave arms if possible.

Each infielder has his designated area, but he may take the play out of his area if he has taken charge of the play. NOTE: Especially on windy days, do not call for play too soon.

On questionable pop flies around the mound area and after one or more infielders has called for the play, the pitcher then calls the last name of the fielder he thinks is in the best position to make the play.

The catcher must not give up on pop flies too quickly.

All pop flies directly behind the first and third basemen will be the responsibility of the second baseman and the shortstop.

Index